Early American Civilization and Exploration–1607

VOLUME 1

Other titles in the American History by Era series:

AMERICAN HISTORY BY ERA

Early American Civilization and Exploration–1607

VOLUME 1

Helen Cothran, *Book Editor*

Daniel Leone, *President*
Bonnie Szumski, *Publisher*
Scott Barbour, *Managing Editor*

GREENHAVEN
PRESS®

THOMSON

—★—™

GALE

San Diego • Detroit • New York • San Francisco • Cleveland
New Haven, Conn. • Waterville, Maine • London • Munich

LIBRARY OF CONGRESS CATALOGING-IN-PUBLICATION DATA

Early American civilization and exploration–1607 / Helen Cothran, book editor.
    p. cm. — (American history by era ; v. 1)
Includes bibliographical references (p.) and index.
ISBN 0-7377-1138-8 (alk. paper) — ISBN 0-7377-1137-X (pbk. : alk. paper)
    1. North America—Discovery and exploration. 2. Indians of North America—
History. 3. Explorers—North America—History. I. Helen Cothran. II. Series.
E101 .E37 2003
970.01—dc21
                                                                    2002066464

Printed in the United States of America

CONTENTS

farmed the great mesas of the American Southwest. The Anasazi's disappearance from the Southwest is a mystery.

Chapter 2: A.D. 900 to 1512: First Contact

lizations of the Aztec and Inca. At the center of large population centers, earthen mounds served as platforms for ceremonial buildings, houses for the nobility, and mortuaries where the remains of important persons and many valuables were interred.

3. How Rabbit Fooled Alligator: A Creek Legend

4. Verrazano's Great Mistake

5. The Narváez Debacle

6. The Bay of Horses

Chapter 4: 1537 to 1542: The Second Wave of Exploration

lished San Agustín, a military fort that protected
Spanish interests in the region.

conceptions similar to Heaven and Hell, and they
believed that people could rise from the dead.

8. Juan de Oñate's Colony and the Pueblo
Juan de Oñate, granted all of present-day New
Mexico in 1598, established a Spanish colony in the
Tewa Indian town of San Juan. His colonists forced
the Indians to convert to Catholicism, depleted the
Tewa's scarce resources, and brutally suppressed
any Indian resistance.

During the sixteenth century, events occurred in North America that would change the course of American history. In 1512, Spanish explorer Juan Ponce de León led the first European expedition to Florida. French navigator Jean Ribault established the first French colony in America at Fort Caroline in 1564. Over a decade later, in 1579, English pirate Francis Drake landed near San Francisco and claimed the country for England.

These three seemingly random events happened in different decades, occurred in various regions of America, and involved three different European nations. However, each discrete occurrence was part of a larger movement for European dominance over the New World. During the sixteenth century, Spain, France, and England vied for control of what was later to become the United States. Each nation was to leave behind a legacy that would shape the political structure, language, culture, and customs of the American people.

Examining such seemingly disparate events in tandem can help to emphasize the connections between them and generate an appreciation for the larger global forces of which they were a part. Greenhaven Press's American History by Era series provides students with a unique tool for examining American history in a way that allows them to see such connections. This series divides American history—from the time that the first people arrived in the New World from Asia to the September 11, 2001, terrorist attacks—into nine discrete periods. Each volume then presents a collection of both primary and secondary documents that describe the major events of the period in chronological order. This structure provides students with a snapshot of events occurring simultaneously in all parts of America. The reader can then gain an appreciation for the political, social, and cultural movements and trends that shaped the nation. Students reading about the adventures of individual European explorers, for instance, are invited to consider how such expeditions compared in purpose and consequence to earlier and later expeditions. Rather than simply learning that Ponce de León was the first Spaniard to try to colonize Florida, for example, students can begin to understand his expedition in a larger context. Indeed, Ponce's voyage was an extension of Spain's desire to conquer the Caribbean and Mexico, and his expedition was to inspire other Spanish explorers to head north from Hispaniola and New Spain in search of rich empires to conquer.

Another benefit of studying eras is that students can view a "snapshot" of America at any given moment of time and see the various social, cultural, and political events that occurred simultaneously. For example, during the period between 1920 and 1945, Charles Lindbergh became the first to make a solo transatlantic flight, Babe Ruth broke the record for the most home runs in one season, and the United States dropped the atomic bomb on Hiroshima. Random events occurring in post–Cold War America included the torching of the Branch Davidian compound in Waco, Texas, the emergence of the World Wide Web, and the 2000 presidential election debacle in which ballot miscounts in Florida held up election results for weeks.

Each volume in this series offers features to enhance students' understanding of the era of American history under discussion. An introductory essay provides an overview of the period, supplying essential context for the readings that follow. An annotated table of contents highlights the main point of each selection. A more in-depth introduction precedes each document, placing it in its particular historical context and offering biographical information about the author. A thorough chronology and index allow students to quickly reference specific events and dates. Finally, a bibliography opens up additional avenues of research. These features help to make the American History by Era series an extremely valuable tool for students researching the political upheavals, wars, cultural movements, scientific and technological advancements, and other events that mark the unfolding of American history.

INTRODUCTION

In 1934 the U.S. Congress declared the second Monday in October of each year "Columbus Day." In 1989 then-president George Bush attempted to articulate the nature of this tribute by proclaiming, "On Columbus Day, we pause as a Nation to honor the skilled and courageous navigator who discovered the Americas and in so doing, brought to our ancestors the promise of the New World."[1] In 1992, on the five-hundredth anniversary of Columbus's first voyage to the Americas, the Italian explorer received an even greater memorial: A presidential commission organized a massive celebration in his honor. The festivities included "a trip to Mars by three solar-powered 'space caravels,' the sale of commemorative coins, and a scholarship program designed to 'both honor the achievements of Columbus and encourage young people who embody his spirit and accomplishments to carry forward his legacy into the next century.'"[2]

Not everyone agreed that Columbus's legacy was cause for celebration, however. Indeed, the quincentennial fueled an already heated debate about how Columbus's voyages should be viewed. The American Library Association declared that "Columbus's voyage to America began a legacy of European piracy, brutality, slave trading, murder, disease, conquest and ethnocide, and further, engendered the Native American Holocaust which saw a population of over 5,000,000 American Indians in the land area of the United States decline to about 250,000 by the last decade of the 19th century."[3] The National Council of the Churches of Christ in the USA issued a resolution on May 17, 1990, stating, "In 1992, celebrations of the 500th anniversary of the arrival of Christopher Columbus in the 'New World' will be held. For the descendants of the survivors of the subsequent invasion, genocide, slavery, 'ecocide' and exploitation of the wealth of the land, a celebration is not an appropriate observation of this anniversary."[4]

TEXTBOOK WARS

The uproar over the Columbus quincentennial highlights a much larger debate about European expansion and colonialism in general. On the one hand, most elementary school students are taught that Columbus discovered the Americas and brought enlightenment and Christianity to the New World. Traditional high school textbooks place Columbus's discovery within the context of a greater phenomenon called the age of exploration, a period that includes Ferdinand Magellan's circumnavigation of the globe and Vasco da Gama's rounding of Africa's Cape of Good Hope. Such texts invite readers to consider such explorers as heroes.

On the other hand, many historians and others argue that American textbooks provide a skewed picture of history. They point out that the new lands discovered by the Europeans during the age of exploration were in fact already discovered, explored, and populated. They argue that when the English, French, Spanish, and Portuguese colonized the Americas, they were actually stealing land that belonged to the indigenous people. As historian Howard Zinn puts it, "It was new to [the Europeans]. It wasn't new to the people who were [in America]."[5] These critics contend that American history textbooks are full of lies and provide a Eurocentric view of historical events that virtually ignores the profoundly negative impact that European colonization had on America's aboriginal people. To illustrate their argument, these critics point out that most children learn nothing about the people who lived in North America before 1492; for Americans, history begins with Columbus.

To sort out the arguments about Columbus and the age of exploration, it is necessary to turn back to the time when humans first discovered the land we call the Americas. As it happens, this first discovery occurred many thousands of years before Columbus set foot in the "New World" and many thousands of miles to the north.

CROSSING THE BERING STRAIT

More than ten thousand years ago, the first humans crossed the Bering Strait from Asia into what is present-day Alaska. The migration occurred during the Pleistocene, which was characterized by extensive glaciation. Anthropologists theorize that the first Americans might have been able to walk from Asia to North America on a land bridge. Such a bridge might have been exposed when the oceans receded as a result of glaciation. Another theory holds that the strait froze over and the migrants simply traveled over the ice. It is also possible that the first Americans sailed from northern Asia to Alaska—a distance of less than sixty miles. In any case, over the next centuries waves of migrants gradually dispersed southward and within two to three thousand years had reached the southernmost tip of South America.

During the thousands of years that these first Americans spread over the two continents before Columbus's arrival, they established several great civilizations. The Aztec Empire in Mexico and the Inca Empire in Peru were at their height of development during the sixteenth century when the first Spanish explorers arrived in Central and South America. These spectacular empires astounded the first Spanish explorers. Indeed, in the eyes of the Spaniards, the population centers of these civilizations in many ways surpassed the great European cities of London and Paris. The discovery of these rich empires—which the Spaniards promptly sacked, plundered, and destroyed— would inspire other explorers to head north to what is now the United States in search of similar civilizations to conquer. Although they would not find the degree of material wealth discovered to the south, early explorers to North America did encounter advanced civilizations.

THE TEMPLE-MOUND BUILDERS

Although other early cultures in the Americas might not have achieved the sophistication that marked the Aztec and Inca worlds, there were, nonetheless, impressive civilizations to the north. For example, the Mississippian civilization—which lasted from A.D. 500 to around 1600—was characterized by huge population centers—sometimes containing as many as seventy-five thousand people—ruled by a single chief or several chiefs. Power was centralized, and there was strong social stratification between chiefs and commoners. Archaeologists consider the work of those chiefs to represent the utmost in political and social organization north of Mexico.

Mississippian culture is most notable for its spectacular temple mounds, many of which contained millions of cubic feet of earth. Mounds served as platforms for ceremonial buildings, houses of the nobility, or mortuaries for ranking persons. Temples contained many treasures, including shells, pearls, feathers, and life-size statues of men and women. Conch shells discovered in the tombs were engraved with designs of humans dressed in animal costumes, winged-and-horned rattlesnakes, and geometric shapes. Other objects found in burial mounds include axes, swords, pipes, and human figures of polished stone. Archaeologists have also discovered polychrome pottery shaped like birds, frogs, dogs, and people. Many archaeologists believe that the artists of the period did not consider themselves to be artists but rather craftsmen creating utilitarian objects. These objects were made to placate the gods, carry food and water, kill game, and show reverence for the dead. This art reveals a well-established culture in which humans lived in harmony with nature.

Perhaps the most spectacular temple-mound society was Cahokia in what is now Collinsville, Illinois. The village extended for six miles and contained eighty-five temple and burial mounds, some of which contained more than 4 million cubic feet of earth. According to anthropologist Timothy R. Pauketat and archaeologist Thomas E. Emerson, "Cahokia, more than any of its contemporary 'Mississippian' neighbors, was a vortex of native social, political, economic, and religious activity."[6] Residents of Cahokia were excellent farmers who successfully cultivated several kinds of crops, the main one being corn. This ability to successfully grow their own food permitted the people to settle down in one place and develop the sophisticated culture found at Cahokia. Cahokia's dominance lasted from about A.D. 1000 to 1250, and scholars are still debating why such an advanced civilization disappeared.

Later generations of mound builders—most notably the Coosa and Calusa—were encountered by the first Spanish explorers to North America. The Spaniards were impressed with the native people's accomplishments, and, in particular, marveled at the enormity and magnificence of the temple mounds. Garcilaso de la Vega, a chronicler of the 1539 Hernando de Soto expedition, described one of the sacred tombs that the Spaniards discovered: "On the floor along the walls were some wooden benches which were excellently carved, as was everything in that temple; and resting upon these benches were the chests which served as sepulchres for the lifeless bodies of the curacas [chiefs] who had been lords of the province, . . . their children, their brothers and sisters, and their nieces and nephews."[7]

When the Spanish explorers began arriving in the American Southwest during the sixteenth century, they encountered the ancestors of another great civilization, the Anasazi. The Anasazi were ancient people who occupied the Four Corners region of the southwestern United States from around A.D. 200 to 1300. Around the year 1050, scattered groups of people began to congregate in large population centers. The most impressive of these centers was located at Chaco Canyon in present-day New Mexico, Mesa Verde in Colorado, and Kayenta in Arizona. According to the *American Heritage Book of Indians*, this time of concentration "opened up a Golden Age of Pueblos, an era lasting through the 13th century."[8]

During this golden age, the Anasazi developed a high level of architectural expertise. They erected elaborate multistoried dwellings, which the first Spanish explorers were later to call pueblos. Perhaps the most spectacular example of Anasazi architecture can been seen in the cliff dwellings at Mesa Verde. Here, an entire city was built beneath the shelter of a cliff. This location was intelligently chosen: In summer, the shadows from the cliff kept the residents cool; in winter, the cliff overhang protected the people from snow. In addition, the winter sun—which is lower in the sky than the summer sun—hit the dwellings, warming them. Archaeologists also speculate that such a location may have been chosen because it was easily defended. The Anasazi cut steps into the cliff that they could use to climb to the mesa above, where they grew crops, primarily corn. This amazing cliff city includes many multistoried "apartment buildings" and kivas, which were underground chambers, usually round or key-shaped, used by men for ceremonial purposes.

Architectural achievements were not limited to cliff palaces. Pueblo Bonito at Chaco Canyon contained free-standing dwellings that could house more than one thousand people and covered more than three acres. In fact, according to the *American Heritage Book of Indians*, Pueblo Bonito "was the world's largest 'apartment house' until a larger one was erected in New York in 1882."[9]

Perhaps most impressive about the Anasazi is their achievement of such a high level of civilization despite extreme climatic conditions. The climate was dry on the Colorado Plateau, which necessitated clever agricultural techniques in order to grow the food that allowed for a sedentary existence. The Anasazi built dams and canals that enabled them to divert precious water to their crops. They also learned how to hybridize, plant, and cultivate corn to ensure its survival even in drought conditions. In addition, the Anasazi crafted containers for storing food and water that were crucial to their survival during the dry months.

Because of their sedentary lifestyle and the necessity of storing food and water, the Anasazi made many kinds of storage vessels. The first Anasazi people—called the Basket-Makers—made tightly woven baskets with which to hold corn and other foodstuffs. As the people became sedentary, however, it became imperative to have some kind of waterproof containers. In consequence, the Anasazi began making pottery. At the height of their pottery-making skills, the Anasazi were crafting pots that far exceeded simple functionality. Indeed, such pottery was elevated to an art form.

Unfortunately, the arid climate of the American Southwest seems to have eventually proved to be too much of a hardship for the people living in the great population centers. An inspection of tree rings indicates that a drought of twenty-three years occurred between 1276 and 1299. This was a catastrophe that no amount of agricultural know-how could mitigate. Anthropologists speculate that during this period the Anasazi had also begun being harassed by roving bands of Apache and Navajo, the latter having given the Anasazi their name, which in Navajo means "enemies." Whatever the reasons, by the 1300s the Anasazi had deserted their great cities and scattered across the Southwest.

THE DESCENDANTS OF THE ANASAZI: THE HOPI AND THE ZUNI

Although the golden age of pueblos was over, the people themselves became absorbed in nearby populations and became the ancestors of the modern people now known as the Hopi and the Zuni. These are the indigenous people whom Spanish explorer Francisco Vásquez de Coronado encountered in 1540 as he traveled into the Southwest from Mexico looking for the Seven Cities of Gold. As it turned out, the Seven Cities were Zuni pueblos containing no gold, gems, or other such treasures valued by the Spaniards. Indeed, Coronado was so disappointed that he ultimately wrote the king of Spain to say that he was aborting the journey because his expedition had been a failure.

Because the explorer's goal was to find riches, Coronado could not appreciate the civilization he encountered. The Pueblo—as the Hopi and the Zuni are called—were a unique people. At a time when many other Indians were roving the great expanse of continent in search of game, the Hopi and the Zuni had settled down into democratic communities sustained by a highly effective agricultural system. The Pueblo had no kings or chiefs, only high priests who, like the other men, were farmers. Among some Pueblo groups, the people were divided into two birthright groups: the Summer People and the Winter People. Each group took turns running the town for half a year. In some pueblos, men owned the houses and everything in them, but in others, women held the property. In some groups, people were expected to participate in the religious activities dictated by the clan; in others, people were allowed to choose their own activities. Essentially, the Hopi and the Zuni acted in accordance with the needs and wishes of the group, making Pueblo communities highly democratic.

Perhaps the phrase that best characterizes the Pueblo people is "everything in moderation." They did not drink nor engage in the ecstatic religious vision quests that their Mexican neighbors did. For example, rather than consume jimsonweed in order to induce hallucinations, the Pueblo used the narcotic as an anesthetic. The Pueblo were industrious and peaceful people who revered nature. Their reverence for nature can be seen in their religious practices. They strove to live in concert with the natural environment and engaged in sun, rain, and corn rituals. In one ritual, they presented a newborn baby to the sun; in another, they thoroughly cleaned their pueblos at harvest time to make them worthy of receiving the corn. Above all, religion was a way to enforce living the right way.

From the Pueblo to the Temple-Mound Builders, from the Inca Empire to the Aztec, the Americas were rich with vibrant civilizations. The people had ancestors, traditions, religions, homes, and property. They built cities, raised crops, created art, had children, and reared them according to deeply held beliefs. The continents had a long and varied history dating back thousands of years to the time when the first Americans walked across the Bering Strait into the New World.

For centuries, however, an entire population across the Atlantic Ocean remained ignorant of their neighbors to the West. Unfortunately, when the Europeans did land on the American continents and discovered the diverse people who lived there, they did not see them as people having rights. The European explorers' treatment of the indigenous people of the Americas was shaped by economic, religious, and political factors stemming from the situation in Europe at that time.

EUROPE AND THE AGE OF EXPLORATION

The phrase "gold, God, and glory" reflects the primary motives that shaped the Europeans' behavior toward the indigenous people of the Americas. The main reason that most men set out from their homes in Europe to brave the world's oceans in leaky ships was to gain wealth, spread Christianity, and obtain power and prestige for their homes or adopted nations. Furthermore, these goals had a long history. During the Crusades—which began during the eleventh century and lasted until the thirteenth—Europeans had discovered the riches of the East. The spices, silks, cottons, and other goods that at first were viewed by Europeans as luxuries soon were seen as necessities. Predictably, as demand increased, the prices of these goods rose. Most of the cost had to do with the fact that the goods had to be transported over dangerous land or sea routes from China and India to Europe. Many an adventurous and entrepreneurial sailor dreamed of finding a direct route to Asia, and the sailors were encouraged in these pursuits by powerful European governments.

The main contestants in this race were Holland, Spain, Portugal, France, and England. Whereas in the past European nations primarily battled one another for resources owned by each other, the age of exploration marked a transition to fighting over resources in other parts of the world. Historians J. Michael Allen and James B. Allen write that "beginning about 1500 the history of the world became a history of European expansion."[10] The combatants began competing against one another for control of the seas. Pirating became a lucrative profession and was often backed by the pirates' home nation. For example, England's Queen Elizabeth I encouraged Sir Francis Drake to pirate Spanish vessels loaded with treasure. In 1588 Spain sent the Spanish Armada to invade England, but England had faster, more maneuverable ships and eventually defeated the Spanish.

In this new struggle for power among the European nations, it was Portugal that enjoyed the first victory. Portuguese sailor Vasco da Gama became the first European to reach India by sea by sailing around Africa's Cape of Good Hope during his voyage of 1497–1499. However, because this route was still considered long and dangerous, other explorers continued to search for a more direct route to Asia. Sailors were aided in this enterprise by advances in technology such as improved mapmaking, better navigational equipment, and sturdier ships. Adventurers and wealth seekers from all nations asked their monarchs to finance voyages, and if their own monarchs refused, they simply moved to another country and petitioned that nation's monarchs. Such was the case with Italian sailor Christopher Columbus, who had been turned down by the Portuguese Crown and eventually undertook his journey financed by Spanish monarchs King Ferdinand and Queen Isabelle.

As it turned out, Columbus did not find China or India. At first he thought he had, which was why he called the Caribbean islands the West Indies and their residents Indians. However, Columbus was eventually to realize that he had discovered a new world that lay between Europe and Asia. Even though Columbus did not receive the honors of being the first to find another route to Asia, his voyage was to have an enormous impact on both Europe and the Americas because it opened new continents to powerful European interests. Spain, Portugal, France, and, a little later, England began to vie for control of the new territory. In this struggle for domination, the native inhabitants of the Americas were considered inferiors, impediments, enemies, and slaves.

THE CONQUEST OF THE NEW WORLD

Perhaps Columbus best epitomizes the attitude of European explorers toward the people they encountered in the Americas. In a letter to Lord Raphael Sánchez, one of his patrons, the Italian explorer praised the indigenous people he first met in the New World. According to Columbus, they were "very simple and honest and exceedingly liberal with all they have . . . [and were] men of great deference and kindness."[11] Columbus seems to have respected the natives' guilelessness. However, he quickly perceived that their simplicity would make them easy to exploit. On a more ominous note, Columbus later recorded in his log, "Should your Majesties [the king and queen of Spain] command it, all the inhabitants could be taken away to Castile [Spain], or made slaves on the island. With 50 men we could subjugate them all and make them do whatever we want."[12]

Another example that typifies the spirit of the age was the *requerimiento*, a formal requirement read by Spanish explorers to all Indians. The statement demanded the submission of all Indians to claims of the Crown and the Holy Church. When a Spaniard first approached an Indian village, he would immediately seek out the village leader and read this pronouncement. As no Indians then knew Spanish, and because most people want to hold onto what belongs to them, the villagers would resist efforts by the Spaniards to take over their villages and their precious stores of food. Possessed of the *requerimiento*, the Spaniards believed they had both a moral and a legal right to forcibly take the lands they discovered. In addition, they felt a moral imperative to convert the Indians to Christianity. Both of these goals usually necessitated the brutal and often fatal suppression of Indian rebellions. With their superior weapons, horses, and ferocious dogs, the outnumbered Spaniards were usually successful in routing the Indians from their homes. This process was repeated wherever the Spaniards went. Because the Spanish were the first of the European powers to explore North America, it took no time at all for the native inhabitants to equate all white men with death and destruction.

Another factor that made the European conquest of North America so expeditious was disease. Whereas Europeans had gradually developed immunity to such diseases as smallpox, mumps, and certain strains of flu, the native inhabitants of the relatively disease-free American continents had no immunity to these illnesses. Indians who came in contact with Europeans quickly became ill, and often entire villages were wiped out in a matter of months. In fact, more Indians died from European diseases than from European weapons.

Intertribal warfare also made it easier for the Europeans to vanquish the Indians. Explorers would learn that two tribes were enemies and would quickly exploit the situation by engaging the help of one of the tribes in attacking the other. Of course, once the enemy tribe was routed, the Spaniards would then turn on their allies, killing the men, taking the women as concubines, and looting and burning the village. The combination of superior weapons, disease, and intertribal warfare enabled the outnumbered Europeans to gain control over the continents with surprising speed.

The Spanish search for gold, although successful in Mexico and Peru, largely failed in North America. But the conquistadors still had two other goals to accomplish: God and glory. Indeed, converting the "heathen" to Christianity was frequently lauded as the overarching reason for colonizing the New World. Columbus articulated this aim when he wrote in his log, which was addressed to the king and queen of Spain, "I see and know that these people have no religion whatever, nor are they idolaters. . . . Your Highnesses must resolve to make them Christians. I believe that if this effort commences, in a short time a multitude of peoples will be converted to our Holy Faith."[13] Many well-meaning Franciscan friars came to the Americas along with the colonizers in order to help the Indians accept the Catholic faith. They truly believed that the Indians had no religion and that their souls would go to hell unless they accepted Christianity. Unfortunately, the process of conversion was usually a bloody one. Over time, some missionaries began to deplore the conversion attempts and speak on behalf of the aboriginal people.

One outspoken critic of the Spanish conversion effort was the ordained priest Bartolomé de Las Casas, who came to the Americas as a colonist. During the later years of his life, Las Casas argued that the pacification of the Indians was an appalling act. Although writing about the Spaniards' relations with the Indians in Central and South America and the Caribbean, Las Casas's observations are equally relevant to the situation in North America. Las Casas observed,

> Into this land of meek outcasts there came some Spaniards who immediately behaved like ravening wild beasts, wolves, tigers, or lions that had been starved for many days. . . . Their reason for killing and destroying such an infinite number of souls is that the Christians have an ultimate aim, which is to acquire gold, and to swell themselves with riches in a very brief time and thus rise to a high estate disproportionate to their merits. It should be kept in mind that their insatiable greed and ambition [are] the greatest ever seen in the world.[14]

In fact, many of the missionaries who came to the New World began to doubt both the motives of the Christians and the wisdom of trying to convert a people who already had their own religion.

Should gold and God not prove adequate incitements, there was always glory. Individuals like Columbus were motivated by a desire to raise their status. Columbus's motives can be seen in his agreement with the Spanish monarchs. This agreement, called the Capitulations of Santa Fe, promised the sailor the rank of admiral for life, the title to be passed on in perpetuity to all of his heirs. He was also to be viceroy and governor-general of all the lands he discovered. Although the capitulations brought glory to Columbus, the Spanish monarchs—like the rulers of Spain's enemies—stood to gain more from such an agreement. Should the explorers whom they financed succeed in finding wealthy empires to conquer or a quicker route to China, the monarchs' prestige was sure to grow. The spoils from new lands would increase their larders and enable them to more powerfully contest the efforts of other nations to establish themselves as imperial powers. Discovery of new lands and their colonization extended each nation's power and influence in a world that was quickly becoming smaller.

THE SUCCESS OF EUROPEAN EXPANSION

Generally speaking, the European explorers and the nations they represented achieved "gold, God, and glory" in the Americas. Many explorers and conquistadors did indeed get rich, and to the extent that an ample portion of all explorers' wealth went directly to the monarchs they served, the vying nations also got richer. These nations also obtained wealth from the sugar plantations established in the Caribbean, the traffic in Indian and African slaves needed to work such plantations, and the trade in raw materials such as gold and copper. In addition, during the age of exploration, the Christian god was introduced to two continents. Indeed, the conversion to Christianity proved to be long-lasting, for many of the indigenous people in North, Central, and South America still practice the Catholic faith. Glory, too, came to the European colonial powers. After all, France, England, Spain, and Portugal spread their influence by exporting their languages and cultures to other parts of the world. Canadians speak English and French, Americans speak English, and most people in Central and South America speak Spanish, except for those in Brazil, who speak Portuguese.

This process of exporting cultural, linguistic, and political influence to the New World is only part of the phenomenon that historian Alfred W. Crosby Jr. calls "the Columbian exchange."[15] The Old World explorers' contribution to the process is usually the better-known aspect of the exchange. For their part, the Europeans brought Christianity, horses, and European languages and political systems to the New World. Less noted is the other half of the equation—what the New World gave to the Old. For instance, foods such as corn, potatoes, turkey, chocolate, peppers, and tomatoes came from the New World. Corn and potatoes, in particular, were extremely important contributions because such fare was nutritious and easy to grow.

Critics of the way American history has traditionally been taught are not surprised that most people know what Europeans brought to the New World while few know what gifts the New World made to the Old. This ignorance illustrates the problems that result from a Eurocentric approach to history, they say. They claim that while history books and elementary school teachers are extolling the virtues of the first European explorers to the Americas, they are neglecting—in a sense obliterating—an entire people who were, in the truest sense, Americans. When Columbus is presented as a brave discoverer worthy of extravagant celebrations, hundreds of thousands of people, their history, their accomplishments, and their destruction are ignored.

The debate about Columbus's legacy continues to rage. Suzan Shown Harjo, a Cheyenne-Creek and president of the Morning Star Foundation in Washington, D.C., explained in an October 1991 interview why she was protesting the Columbus quincentenary: "As Native American peoples in this red quarter of Mother Earth, we have no reason to celebrate an invasion that caused the demise of so many of our people and is still causing destruction today. The Europeans stole our land and killed our people."[16] In contrast, Mark Falcoff, resident scholar at the American Enterprise Institute, celebrates Columbus's legacy. He argues, "Without [Columbus's] journey in the first place, the history of humanity might have been very different—and very much darker."[17] Falcoff points to countries where Western influence failed—tumultuous and despotic nations such as Iraq—to illustrate how superior the ideas and values are that Columbus brought with him to America.

Indeed, to some Columbus is a hero, and to others a villain. Some people celebrate the European discovery of the Americas while others contend that the Americas had already been discovered. Some commentators see the colonization of America as the spreading of enlightenment. Others see it as stealing. To be sure, much of the debate about Columbus and the age of exploration centers around the meaning of certain words: *discovery, ownership, land rights, stealing*. What is certain is that the ten-thousand-year evolution of American civilization changed abruptly and forever with Columbus's voyage in 1492.

NOTES

1. Quoted in John Yewell, Chris Dodge, and Jan DeSirey, eds., *Confronting Columbus: An Anthology.* Jefferson, NC: McFarland, 1992, p. 200.

2. Yewell, Dodge, and DeSirey, *Confronting Columbus*, p. 196.

3. Quoted in Yewell, Dodge, and DeSirey, *Confronting Columbus*, p. 196.

4. Quoted in Yewell, Dodge, and DeSirey, *Confronting Columbus*, p. 189.

5. Quoted in Yewell, Dodge, and DeSirey, *Confronting Columbus*, p. 3.

6. Timothy R. Pauketat and Thomas E. Emerson, eds., *Cahokia: Domination and Ideology in the Mississippian World.* Lincoln: University of Nebraska Press, 1997, p. 1.

7. Quoted in Roy S. Dickens Jr., *Of Sky and Earth: Art of the Early Southeastern Indians.* Dalton, GA: Lee Printing, 1982, p. 14.

8. *The American Heritage Book of Indians.* New York: American Heritage, 1961, p. 127.

9. *The American Heritage Book of Indians*, p. 114.

10. J. Michael Allen and James B. Allen, *World History from 1500.* New York: HarperPerennial, 1993, p. 19.

11. Quoted in Yewell, Dodge, and DeSirey, *Confronting Columbus*, p. 67.

12. Quoted in Yewell, Dodge, and DeSirey, *Confronting Columbus*, p. 67.

13. Quoted in Helen Cothran, ed., *The Conquest of the New World.* San Diego: Greenhaven, 2002, p. 9.

14. Quoted in Cothran, *The Conquest of the New World*, p. 51.

15. Quoted in Cothran, *The Conquest of the New World*, p. 13.

16. Quoted in Cothran, *The Conquest of the New World*, p. 15.

17. Quoted in Cothran, *The Conquest of the New World*, p. 4.

Prehistory to A.D. 900: First Inhabitants

CHAPTER 1

THE FIRST INHABITANTS OF THE NEW WORLD

VERA BROWN HOLMES

Vera Brown Holmes was a professor of history at Smith College and author of the book *A History of the Americas, from Discovery to Nationhood*, the source of the following selection. Holmes explains that the first inhabitants of the Americas migrated from Asia to Alaska by crossing the Bering Strait some ten to twenty-five thousand years ago. According to Holmes, these modern humans found themselves in a completely isolated and uninhabited world. Successive generations of people slowly migrated southward, and within two to three thousand years, many had arrived at the southern tip of South America. Holmes writes that when Columbus arrived in 1492, more than thirteen million people lived in the Americas, about one million of those inhabiting North America. However, more recent estimates conclude that more than 100 million people lived in the Americas in 1492, 10 million of them in North America.

The first known inhabitants of the Americas were northern Asiatics of a Mongoloid type, who arrived by way of Alaska in successive waves of immigration across Bering Strait some ten to twenty-five thousand years ago. Striking evidence of at least this degree of antiquity for man in America came in 1926 with a purely chance discovery in an eroding arroyo near Folsom, New Mexico. Here were found a number of flint spear points and scrapers, obviously grooved and chipped by man, lying in close association with the huge bones of a type of bison known to have become extinct at least ten thousand years ago. The soil deposits in which these artifacts and animal bones occurred were of the same distant period. From a study of the region it was clear that man must have been in America early enough to find the now arid high plains still well watered and covered with lush grasses. Here was concrete evidence that the early Americans had known at first hand and hunted with the help of a spear, tipped with a flint point and probably flung with a spear-thrower, the straight-horned Taylor's bison that in great herds had found food and water in the area. Since those first finds, the pathway of the "Folsom hunters" has been traced back through dozens of camp sites across the United States and Canada to a starting point in Alaska. Other archaeological discoveries at Sandía in New Mexico, in Cochise County, Arizona, and elsewhere have served to confirm the view that man had spread over a considerable part of North America at a period not far removed from the close of the last great glaciation. The earliest Americans may actually have seen the retreating continental glaciers! But nowhere have there been found any human remains of the Folsom man himself.

BY SEA, BY ICE, OR BY LAND

Whether a catastrophe in the old homeland or some fundamental change of circumstances, such as the pressure of overpopulation with diminishing food supply, drove these red men forth from northern Asia, we may never know. But we may be sure that they came and enough of them were able to maintain themselves to form the basis of a population for a hemisphere believed hitherto void of human inhabitants. Here probably were the real discoverers of America. It is not exactly known how these first Americans succeeded in crossing the fifty-six miles of ocean that separate America from Asia at the narrowest point. The feat, however, was not a difficult one. On fine days the American shore is clearly visible from the Asiatic coast. The beckoning headlands of Alaska may well have seemed to primitive man, once he had learned to make crude boats, no more unreachable than distant heights along his own shore. The centrally placed Diomede Islands would have helped as stepping stones, leaving the longest stretch of open water a mere twenty-five miles. The Eskimo of today in his primitive skin boat often makes the journey. However, an open-water crossing may not have been necessary. Some of the earliest Americans may have crossed on the drift ice that even today forms large fields north of the strait, and in the more severe winters of that age may have provided an ice bridge. Furthermore, it is possible that a land bridge, over which animals must have come to America in Pleistocene times, may have persisted long enough to permit early man to walk to America over land.

The origin of America's first inhabitants was thus Asiatic, and their advent came at a comparatively late date. Nowhere has there been discovered generally accepted evidence of a really primitive human type, nor are there any anthropoid apes. There have been found in America no human remains that scientists will agree correspond in age to the Heidelberg or Neanderthal man in Europe.

This indicates a unique prehistory for the continent and sets America definitely apart from the Old World where there are numerous traces of man and early simian types in Asia, Europe, and Africa of immense antiquity, in some cases hundreds of thousands of years in the past. The isolation of America and the remoteness of its avenues of approach from the original foci of population in the Old World offer at least a partial explanation why America alone among the continents remained uninhabited so long. Eventually, however, Asiatic man, probably in groups arriving hundreds of years apart and following in the footsteps of such Pleistocene mammals as the bison, the mammoth, the mastodon, the giant sloth, the great beaver, and the wild horse and camel, reached the northwest corner of the American continent and opened the human chapter in the history of the Western Hemisphere.

A DIVERSE PEOPLE MOVES SOUTH

These first American immigrants showed considerable diversity of physical form. While, like their descendants of today, they possessed in common yellow-brown to red-brown skins, high cheekbones, straight coarse black hair, scanty beards and dark eyes that appear oblique, in the more fundamental matters of stature and shape of head there was a good deal of variety. Some were longheads, some were roundheads; some were short in stature, and some were tall. Their culture does not appear to correspond exactly to any Old World classification, though it parallels the Upper Palaeolithic of Europe in time. They depended entirely for food and clothing on hunting the abundant and varied game they found on the continent, on fishing, and on the gathering of roots, seeds, nuts, and fruits. They had no knowledge of agriculture, weaving, pottery, or metals, though perhaps they had learned to make crude baskets and had domesticated the dog. Their principal weapons were the stone club, the spear with its skilfully chipped flint point, probably the spear-thrower, and the harpoon; the bow and arrow perhaps came later. Among their most useful implements were the flint knife, the scraper, the stone axe, and the fire drill. Their religion was probably a mixture of magic and animism. Social organization rested on a basis of blood, kinship, and contiguity, with communal and family responsibility well understood. An aggregation of family groups into a tribe led by a chief was an early gain, a step already taken by the more advanced of the migratory groups or taken soon after arrival in the New World. Of the stage reached in linguistic development among the aborigines, we know very little. If differentiation into a variety of tongues had not already proceeded apace at the time of crossing, divergence into numerous groups took place rapidly afterwards, largely because of the absence of the steadying influence of a written language and because of the ever-widening geographical barriers separating groups in the New World.

Once arrived in Alaska, and finding themselves unopposed by man or too formidable wild animals, the first immigrants soon moved southward either urged on from behind by new hordes or attracted from the bleakness of the first wilderness to the more moderate climate and the prospect of more abundant food ahead. It is of course impossible to follow with any exactness the ebb and flow of the tribes, or the routes pursued. The vanguard of the first immigrants may have reached the isthmus connecting the two American continents within a few hundred years. Here in the tropics the advance southward of the wanderers was slower as the geographical obstacles increased in difficulty, but by the close of two or three thousand years after the migration began, the wave of humanity had probably reached the southern tip of South America.

Through the following ten thousand years the red man lived in America unmolested and uninfluenced by Asia or Europe except by the arrival of new groups of his own people, and troubled only by internal dissension. Even this could hardly have been serious in view of the almost unlimited space available. . . .

THIRTEEN MILLION STRONG

When Columbus arrived the American continents were inhabited from the Arctic to the Antarctic. Considering how much was virgin forest, the habitable areas were probably not too sparsely peopled, although there are few materials from which to arrive at any reliable estimate of numbers. Guesses run from eight and a half to fifty millions. A recent, careful statistical study places the probable number of natives in both North and South America at the time of the Conquest at 13,385,000 of which number 1,000,000 is assigned to the region north of Mexico, 4,500,000 to Mexico, 6,785,000 to South America. Such a low estimate is, however, disputed by many specialists whose figures for specific areas point to a much higher aggregate. It is clear that the Indian population was by no means evenly distributed. Certain favorable regions, such as Mexico, Central America, Peru, Colombia, and the Mississippi area, were thickly settled. Others were very thinly peopled. In general the regions of greatest population were those of highest culture.

THE FIRST OLD WORLD SAILORS ARRIVE IN AMERICA

BARRY FELL

Barry Fell claims in the following selection that Leif Erickson and Christopher Columbus were not the first Old World sailors to discover America. He contends that increasing archeological evidence—such as ancient writing, marked graves, and Druid circles—indicates that ancient Celts, Basques, Libyans, and Egyptians sailed to the New World twenty-five hundred years ago. According to Fell, these early explorers used the trade winds to make their way to the Caribbean, and from there, sailed north to present-day New England, where they intermingled with American Indians. A Harvard biologist turned epigrapher, Barry Fell is the author of *America B.C.: Ancient Settlers in the New World*, the source of this selection.

There is more to America's past than appears upon the surface. A strange unrest is apparent among many of the younger historians and archeologists of the colleges and universities, a sense that somehow a very large slice of America's past has mysteriously vanished from our public records. For how else can we explain the ever-swelling tally of puzzling ancient inscriptions now being reported from nearly all parts of the United States, Canada, and Latin America?

The inscriptions are written in various European and Mediterranean languages in alphabets that date from 2,500

Barry Fell, *America B.C.: Ancient Settlers in the New World*, New York, Pocket Books, 1989. Copyright © 1989 by Pocket Books. Reproduced by permission of Time Books, a division of Random House, Inc.

years ago, and they speak not only of visits by ancient ships, but also of permanent colonies of Celts, Basques, Libyans, and even Egyptians. They occur on buried temples, on tablets and on gravestones and on cliff faces. From some of them we infer that the colonists intermarried with the Amerindians, and so their descendants still live here today.

There was once a time when such finds were attributed to the misguided folly of uprooted colonists from Europe, to forgers or cranks fabricating tradition for a society that has none. But skepticism changed to bewilderment when it was discovered that American inscriptions, some of them known for a century or more, turn out to have been written in ancient scripts of a type only recently deciphered in Europe or North Africa. Thus the truth has slowly come to light, ancient history is inscribed upon the bedrock and buried stone buildings of America, and the only hands that could have inscribed it were those of ancient people. America, as we now realize, is a treasure house of records of man's achievement upon the high seas in bygone ages. Even more so are our inscribed rocks and tablets a heritage from a forgotten era of colonization. They tell us of settlers who came from the Old World and who remained to become founding fathers of some of the Amerindian nations.

These ancient writings can easily be classified into some half dozen styles, each now known to be associated with one or other of several ancient peoples whose languages have been in part recovered. New inscriptions are being discovered almost every day, from localities thousands of miles apart, usually under circumstances that preclude any possibility of fraud. . . .

CELTIC COLONIZERS

These remarkable facts began to come to light in 1975 in the course of an archeological survey of New Hampshire and Vermont. Numerous inscriptions among the ruins attest the vitality of a Celtic civilization in pagan times and tell a wonderful story of how European traders lived during the Bronze and Iron Ages. . . .

About three thousand years ago bands of roving Celtic mariners crossed the North Atlantic to discover, and then to colonize, North America. They came from Spain and Portugal, by way of the Canary Islands, sailing the trade winds as Columbus also was to do long afterward. The advantage of this route is that the winds favor a crossing from east to west, but for Celts accustomed to a temperate climate it had the one drawback that it led them to the tropical West Indies, no place for northerners. So although their landfall lay in the Caribbean, it was on the rocky coasts and mountainous hinterlands of New England that most of these wanderers finally landed, there to establish a new European kingdom which they called *Iargalon*, "Land Beyond the Sunset." They built villages and temples, raised Druids' circles and buried their dead in marked graves. They were still there in the time of Julius Caesar, as is attested by an inscribed monolith on which the date of celebration of the great Celtic festival of Beltane (Mayday) is given in Roman numerals appropriate to the reformed Julian calendar introduced in 46 B.C.

In the wake of the Celtic pioneers came the Phoenician traders of Spain, men from Cadiz who spoke the Punic tongue, but wrote it in the peculiar style of lettering known as Iberian script. Although some of these traders seem to have settled only on the coast, and then only temporarily, leaving a few engraved stones to mark their visits or record their claims of territorial annexation, other Phoenicians remained here and, together with Egyptian miners, became part of the Wabanaki tribe of New England. Further south, Basque sailors came to Pennsylvania and established a temporary settlement there, leaving however no substantial monuments other than grave markers bearing their names. Further south still, Libyan and Egyptian mariners entered the Mississippi from the Gulf of Mexico, penetrating inland to Iowa and the Dakotas, and westward along the Arkansas and Cimarron Rivers, to leave behind inscribed records of their presence. Norse and Basque visitors reached the Gulf of St. Lawrence, introducing various mariners' terms into the language of the northern Algonquian Indians. Descendants of these visitors are also to be found apparently among the Amerindian tribes, several of which employ dialects derived in part from the ancient tongues of Phoenicia and North Africa.

The Celts seem first to have settled near the mouths of rivers of New England, as at North Salem on a branch of the Merrimac River in southern New Hampshire. At some time they ascended the Connecticut River, sailing as far north as Quechee, Vermont, where a western branch of the river joins the main stream through a precipitous gorge. Attracted doubtless by the seclusion of the uplands beyond the gorge, the Celts turned westward and colonized the hanging valleys of the Green Mountains. Quechee, incidentally, perpetuates the ancient Gaulish pronunciation of the Celtic word *quithe,* meaning chasm or pit, and the river that flows through the gorge, the Ottauque-chee, similarly is an Amerindian rendering of the Celtic name meaning Waters-of-the-Chasm.

In the secluded valleys and on the hilltops, the priests (or Druids) erected the temples and circles of standing stones required by their religious beliefs, using, like their European cousins, the great stone boulders left upon the land by the retreating glaciers at the end of the ice age. On these stones they cut their inscriptions, using the ancient Celtic alphabet called *Ogam.*

PAGAN INSCRIPTIONS PRESERVED

In Europe the Celts doubtless did the same, but when Christianity came to the Celts the priests caused all the ancient pagan inscriptions to be erased, replaced by Christian Ogam, or left blank, while all the offending fertility paraphernalia were totally destroyed.

Not so in America. Here Christianity never came to the Celts, their old pagan inscriptions remain intact, and a host of giant stone phalluses characterize the places of worship. Here we may yet see and read the ancient inscriptions of the rite of initiation to manhood, and see the sites of ritual worship of the powers of fertility in nature. In short, we have preserved in North America the oldest phases of religious thought and action of European man, of which only the merest traces have survived in Europe itself.

The consequences of these discoveries for archeology and history are, of course, immeasurable. As one historian, Professor Norman Totten, has pointed out, it means that 2,500 years of American prehistory must now be transferred to history; for history begins when writing begins, and we now have the oldest written documents of our nation, and the names of the men who wrote them. For archeology a whole new view is called for. During the past hundred years the belief that no European settled America before Leif Eriksson or Columbus has grown from an hypothesis into a firmly rooted dogma.

For European archeology, where more liberal views as to the antiquity of the Celts have been developing in recent years, the new discoveries in America may be expected to bring a flow of information on such topics as the dates of construction of megalithic buildings, as well as on the purposes for which they were used, and the gods whose rites were once performed within their precincts. For in as much as no Christian priests came to expunge the pagan inscriptions from the megalithic monuments of New England, America's surviving records may well supply the key to discovering who built the corresponding structures in Europe, where no trace remains of inscriptions made before the coming of Christianity.

HISTORY DISTORTED

When we reflect upon the events of the past two centuries of America's nationhood, we perceive that the course of British and American history is shaped like the letter Y. The lower upright of the Y represents the common stream of Europe's cultural heritage, reading upward until we reach the fork of the Y, which represents 1776. Thereafter America and Britain part company, each to pursue a separate path toward whatever destiny may lie in store.

Now it is an indisputable fact that not only has the history of the two English-speaking nations bifurcated like the arms of the Y, but also the *teaching of history* in the schools and colleges of the two nations has followed a similar divergence. British children continue to learn the history of Britain from the remotest stone-age era, through the Celts, the Roman invaders, the Saxon invasions, the Norman invasion, and so on through the middle ages into the present era. American children, on the other hand, use history books which (to judge by the examples that teachers have given me) begin with an account of the benighted state of Europe in 1492 and lead directly, as you turn the first page, to a portrait of Christopher Columbus, followed by an account of his daring exploits and discoveries.

Here you have in a nutshell the difference in approach to history as presented in the schools that most people attend on either side of the Atlantic. For the European, history begins in vague, remote, and romantic mists of antiquity and slowly emerges into the brighter illumination of more recent time. For the American, history begins with the crash of cymbals as great and famous men stride onto the stage, fully documented or so nearly so that one might be pardoned for thinking that their birth certificates and social security cards are stored in the national archives in Washington. Two English humorists, in the book *1066 and All That,* suggested some years ago that there are only two dates in history that British people can remember—55 B.C., when Julius Caesar landed in Britain, and 1066, when

William the Conqueror conquered. It is their mock-serious thesis that since the common man in Britain remembers no other event well enough to date it, no other events exist in British history! I suspect that an analogous satire on American history would have discovered essentially the same thing, except that the two dates every American remembers are 1492 and 1776. Hence there can be no American history prior to 1492, *quod erat demonstrandum.*

Of course the argument is false, but it does contrive to point out, in a blundering way, the nature of certain profound differences in the view of history as seen from the two sides of the Atlantic.

THE FIRST POLYNESIANS ARRIVE IN HAWAII

APA PRODUCTIONS

In the following selection, APA Productions describes how Polynesians from the Marquesas and Tahiti islands sailed in dug-out canoes to Hawaii between A.D. 500 and 1300. These brave sailors became the first settlers of the Hawaiian Islands, which were then pristine and disease-free. According to APA Productions, the Polynesians established a caste society that was ruled by chiefs. These chiefs upheld the islands' systematic laws with force, sometimes sacrificing the accused as examples to others. Many chiefs brutally abused their power, but others ruled wisely, with a mind toward protecting Hawaii's fragile natural resources. APA Productions publishes *Insight* travel guidebooks, including *Hawaii*, from which this excerpt was taken.

T he homely speckled plover, also referred to as the American golden plover, doesn't *just* fly to Hawaii. He also wends his way as far south and southwest as the Marquesas, Tahiti and New Zealand. For more than 3,000 miles, save for an occasional pit stop in Hawaii, Christmas Island and other more obscure landing strips in Oceania, the little plover's heart and wings beat rhythmically through Pacific storms, wind-currents and cloud banks until he finds a home in the Central Pacific or South Seas. Once there, the plover spends nine to ten months fattening up on crustaceans, snails and insects, then, mysteriously, flaps away on an annual return journey to Alaska and Siberia at their warmest.

SAILING AFTER THE PLOVER

Ancient seafaring Polynesians of the Marquesas and Society groups no doubt observed the comings and goings of this curious golden-backed bird. And they probably wondered just where the touring *kolea* was going every late spring. Certainly not somewhere back of nowhere. Like we humans of the 20th Century, they didn't believe that such a fragile bird could fly too far without food, rest and water. Their wonder fueled speculation, and this bird—and other unexplainable natural phenomena—inspired the launching of northerly expeditions of discovery.

In seaworthy, double-hulled canoes embellished with *aumakua,* carved spirit allies, these water-wary islanders set out in pursuit of the plover and other signs of land to the north. They were led in their quest by birds, but also by leaping dolphin, prevailing winds, ocean currents, shifting cloud masses and, most reliably, stars.

Timid Western man waited until the 15th Century and later before daring to set out on ocean journeys of any significant latitude. However, anthropologists believe that Polynesians were navigating their sturdy sea canoes over distances of 1,000 miles or more prior to 500 A.D. They used absolutely no navigating instruments, relying instead on maritime instincts, their eyes, stars and the aforementioned birds and other natural phenomena.

"Even today," report Bernice Pauahi Bishop Museum astronomers Will Kyselka and George Bunton, "the Marquesans use stars to orient themselves in the 120-mile trip from the north to south islands." The highly competent explorer-navigator Captain James Cook, who first sailed to the South Pacific in 1768 to 1771 to "observe the transit of Venus" for the British Admiralty and Royal Society, watched in a seaman's awe as Tahitians took eyeball bearings on stars and ploughed ahead into uncertain seas.

Based on observational-astronomical data accumulated over the years, it has been established that Polynesians made the 2,000-mile-plus run from their South Seas home to Hawaii by trailing the plover, riding "down-hill" tradewinds and fixing on two key stars—Sirius and Arcturus. As Bunton and Kyselka note, "Sirius, the brightest star in the sky, passed almost directly over Tahiti and Raiatea (also called *Hawa'iti*). The present position of Sirius with respect to the equator has changed very little from that of the ancient days of Polynesian voyaging. Arcturus, called by the Hawaiians *Hoku-le'a* and noted for its bright redness off the Big Dipper's handle, presently passes over the northern end of the island of Hawaii. At the time of the great voyaging it passed over the island of Kauai."

A LAND OF FIRE AND GNOMES

However they fixed their first courses, the first discoverers and settlers of Hawaii are believed to have been Polynesian natives of the Marquesas Islands, who arrived in Hawaii sometime between 500 and 800 A.D. Early Marquesan landfalls and settlings in Hawaii have been determined by the carbon dating and comparison of fishhooks and adzes found in Hawaiian and Marquesan living sites of approximately the same period.

About 500 or 600 years later, sometime between 1100 and 1300 A.D., similar central Polynesian fleets from the Society, or Tahitian, Islands, began arriving in the land they referred to in Tahiti as *Hawai'ia*—or "Burning Hawaii," which was believed to be a reference to Hawaii's volcanoes. Scholars have speculated that this second wave of Polynesians subjugated the earlier Marquesans and/or drove them north in the Hawaiian chain until they were either assimilated as slaves or completely destroyed. These conquered Marquesans may have been the *manahune*, or *menehune*, mentioned in early Hawaiian and Tahitian chants. The term *manahune* was used haughtily and derisively in the Tahitian homeland to refer to slaves or plebeian castes, but its meaning changed through the centuries to mean, probably sarcastically, a group of mysterious gnomes or dwarfs who lived in the Hawaiian Islands at the time of the great Tahitian migrations.

But gnomes or no gnomes, both Polynesian groups brought to the Hawaiian Archipelago a common basic language, similar foods, related cultural peculiarities and synonymous myths, traditions and gods. They were basically of the same strong Polynesian stock which populated all the island realms throughout the Central and South Seas.

It was the Tahitians, however, who are credited with bequeathing the name *Hawai'i*, which was first given to the major Big Island of Hawaii and later to this island region in general.

As the Polynesian bard Kama-hua-lele chanted in centuries

past: "Behold *Hawai'i*, an island, a people/The people of *Hawai'i* are the offspring of Tahiti."

ORIGIN OF THE WORD *HAWAII*

Sir Peter Buck, the eminent half-Maori ethnologist who served as director of Hawaii's Bernice Pauahi Bishop Museum from 1936 until his death in 1951, explains the origin of the word *Hawaii* in his 1938 book *Vikings of the Pacific*. He notes that in ancient times "the headquarters of the Polynesian main body was established in the largest island of the leeward group of Tahiti, named *Havai'i* after an ancient homeland."

As Havai'i-based fleets set out to settle the Society Islands, Samoa, Tonga, Fiji, Hawaii and New Zealand—among other scattered places in the Pacific—they established colonies which they often named after their home port-island. . . .

ANCIENT HAWAII

When the first Polynesian dug-out canoes were beached on Hawaii's shores—probably first at or near South Point on the Big Island—these islands were as close to being an unspoiled Eden-Shangrila-Bali Hai as had ever been discovered on earth. Biologists say much of the land was somewhat barren, dusty and largely host to scrub plants, but thriving here and there were some 2,200 kinds of higher plants that occur only in the Hawaiian Islands and nowhere else. The islands' undisturbed shoreline reefs and lagoons, fern forests, rich alluvial plains, and well-watered valleys and highlands were verily splashing, crawling and blooming with what had evolved into Hawaii's indigenous flora, fauna, birds and marine life.

"Most visitors and many residents of the State are not aware of Hawaii's unique plants and see very few of them," writes an author in the University of Hawaii's *Atlas of Hawaii*. "The coconuts, orchids, sugarcane, and pineapples of the tourist advertisements are recent immigrants to Hawaii, neither native nor unique. (And) native plants are common today only in such remote places as the headwalls of deep valleys, on steep cliffs, and on mountain ridges and peaks." However, of Hawaii's 2,200 endemic plants, about 30 percent are considered "endangered," or threatened by extinction, most of them the weaker victims of introduced plant species.

When the first Marquesans arrived in Hawaii, they found some 67 varieties of endemic Hawaiian birds (about 23 of which are now believed extinct), including large fowl such as the *koloa* (the Hawaiian duck) and *nene* (the Hawaiian goose). But astonishingly, neither amphibia (frogs, newts and the like), nor reptiles, nay, not even pesky mosquitos, lice, fleas, flies or gnats were on hand to bug them. And for nearly a thousand years, until mariners began arriving from the East and West bearing common and social diseases, most of the world's debilitating and lethal germs were also absent. These islands were a pristine place, patiently and naively awaiting the introduction of pestilence and disease.

Among higher animal order representatives, the Polynesians found only two endemic mammals—a small bat, the so-called hoary bat (*Lasiurus cinereus*), which had somehow migrated from either North or South America, and the monk seal (*Monachus Schauinslandi*), a relative of seals previously found in the Caribbean and Mediterranean. The hoary bat, known as the *ope'ape'a* to Hawaiians, still swoops in and out of Big Island nights in the vicinity of Kilauea Crater, but the monk seal, which now survives only in Hawaii, rarely ventures near populated islands for a peek at the colorful jet-set mammals who nearly slaughtered him into extinction for his skin and oil during the 19th Century.

ORAL TRADITIONS

Animal and plant life systems in old Hawaii were very fragile indeed, but how could they be otherwise in what is probably the most perfect climate on earth. Hawaii's environment was then—and still is today—a balmy, mellifluous mix of sunshine, misty rainbows, and regular northeasterly tradewinds which act as one of the planet's finest natural air-conditioning systems.

The first Polynesians from the south, however, immediately upset this finite ecological balance. They fortunately had not yet been exposed to many of the diseases and pests we take for granted these days, but they arrived bearing several forms of domestic foodstuff. In their caches were dogs, pigs and chickens (all three for eating), and, probably unintentionally, the first Hawaiian menace, stowaway Hawaiian rats (*Rattus exulans*). To supplement their diet, the first Hawaiians also introduced the starchy tuber staple known as *taro* (from which the grey, pasty mush called *poi* is made), coconuts, bananas, yams, *kukui* candlenuts, wild ginger, breadfruit and sugarcane. Plus utility plants, such as the *wauke*, the paper mulberry (*Broussonetia papyrifera*), which was beaten and sunbleached into *kapa* (bark-cloth), and the *ti* (*Cordyline terminalis*), a lily relative whose roots and leaves are still used as wrapping and matting, and to make *hula* skirts and a liquor called *ti*-root *okolehao*.

But more important than food and fiber stuffs, the Polynesians brought in their minds a remarkable collection of cultural and religious traditions which were directed at the animate and inanimate spirits who ruled their visions of the world and universe.

Most of what we know about "precontact" Hawaii is contained in poetic oral traditions, known to the Hawaiians as *mele*. In these *mele*, the Hawaiians' *kupuna*—or ancestors—passed on to their descendants all they knew of their history. Various aspects of physical and spiritual life—from the trivial to the momentous—were reported in this unwritten literature of family genealogies, myths and day-to-day human experiences. . . .

The Hawaiians had developed into one of the most complex "Stone Age" cultures ever encountered by outside and "civilized" observers.

THE KAPU WAY OF LIFE

Hawaiian life was simple but remarkably subtle and regulated under systematic laws known as *kapu*. *Kapu*, a variation of the Tahitian word *tapu* (or taboo), directed daily life and caste relationships. A hereditary group of *alii*, or noblemen, dominated hereditary *makaainana*, or commoners, and there was no way short of revolution that tightly circumscribed *kapu* and bloodlines could be crossed. A common penalty for a *kapu* violation was execution by being stoned, clubbed, strangled, or being buried or burned alive. Sometimes a *kapu*-breaker was singled out merely as a convenient sacrificial victim, say when a chief wanted to appease a certain god, but usually he was sacrificed to graphically exemplify what might happen to other would-be *kapu* transgressors. *Kapu*-breakers, however, were provided with a place of last resort, similar to biblical cities of refuge, where they could seek sanctuary and live unmolested, whatever their crime. These places of refuge, called *pu'uhonua*, had to be reached by a law-breaker before he was caught by a chief's pursuing warriors. A good example of a *pu'uhonua* is located on a lava promontory at Honaunau, Kona, on the Big Island of Hawaii.

This intricate *kapu* system directly or indirectly affected every aspect of Hawaiian life—from birth to death—until it was overthrown in 1819 by the Hawaiian King Kamehameha II. But until their abolition more than 40 years after the arrival in 1778 of

the British Captain James Cook, *kapu* precepts effectively protected the powers of Hawaiian kings and their underlings.

The Hawaiian scholar-historian David Malo recounted that
a person could be put to death for merely allowing his shadow
to fall upon the house of a *kapu* chief, or for passing through that
chief's stockade or doorway, or entering the house before
changing his *malo* loincloth, or by appearing there with his head
smeared with mud.

"Even if there were no fence surrounding the *alii's* residence,
only a mark or faint scratch in the ground hidden by the grass,
and a man were to overstep this line unwittingly, not seeing it,
he would be put to death . . ." Malo wrote.

More common *kapu* declared that women could not eat pork,
coconuts, bananas and shark meat, nor could they eat with men,
or vice-versa. Also, certain seasons were established (as con-
servation measures) for the gathering or catching of scarce foodstuffs; and sometimes sporting chiefs kapued certain surfing
spots for their personal and exclusive pleasure.

GOOD AND BAD CHIEFS

Some *kapu* were instigated by Machiavellian chiefs, priests or
influential court retainers under the guise of religion, or to ar-
rogantly and tyrannically oppress a person or group of people;
but many of the laws were simply of a conservative or rationing
nature, designed—much as are modern wildlife regulations—
to protect resources from human greed, misuse and pollution.

As Malo notes, "There was a great difference between chiefs.
Some were given to robbery, spoliation, murder, extortion, rav-
ishing," but others (he cites Kamehameha I as an example)
"conducted themselves properly" and "looked after the peace
of the land."

One Hawaiian *moi*, or king, who was immortalized in song
and dance as having been wise and peace-loving was the
"mountain monarch" Umi-a-Liloa, who reigned from about
1490 to 1521. A chant recorded by Fornander reported that:

> When peace and quiet reigned in the government of
> Hawaii under Umi-a-Liloa, his name became famous
> from Hawaii to Kauai. No king was like unto him in
> the administration of his government; he took care of
> the old men and the old women and orphans; he had
> regard for the people also; there were no murders and
> thievings.

The French historian M. Jules Remy wrote in a book about Umi (*Tales of a Venerable Savage*) that the *moi* Umi was so powerful that wherever he went, his followers preceded him and literally devastated the countryside to announce his pending arrival. It was a royal Hawaiian custom which Umi did not personally appreciate, or as Remy recounts:

> It was a settled custom in Hawaiian antiquity for the numerous attendants of the chiefs, when they traveled through a settlement to cut down cocoanut trees, devastate plantations, and commit all sorts of havoc injurious to the interests of the owners or cultivators. To avoid a sort of scourge which attached itself to the steps of the monarch, Umi went and settled in the mountains, so that the depredations of the people of his house might not cause the tears of the people to flow . . .

As aforementioned, many heavy-handed—and benevolent—administrative tactics were attributable to the chiefs' ministers, called the *kalaimoku*, the high priests or *kahuna nui*, and various upper, middle or low-ranking *alii*. These royalists were influenced, in turn, by staff specialists of the realm—craftsmen, priests, medicine men, artisans, teachers and other wise men—who were collectively known as *kahuna*. These upper castes manipulated the vast working class, known as the *makaainana*, and an "untouchable" minority of outcasts called the *kauwa*. The *kauwa*, a pariah group of people who lived apart from the rest of Hawaiian society, were sometimes marked by tatooing of their foreheads and often were summarily conscripted as sacrificial victims by *kahuna* and executioners (the *mu*) in charge of such "religious" procurements.

Sacrifices—only sometimes of human life—were made to any of hundreds of deities in the Hawaiian-Polynesian pantheon, but the four most powerful gods of Hawaiian Polynesia were always *Ku, Kane, Lono* and *Kanaloa* (known in Tahitian as *Tu, Tane, Rongo* and *Tangaroa*).

THE ANASAZI: ANCIENT PEOPLE OF THE ROCK

DONALD G. PIKE

In the following selection, Donald G. Pike describes the Anasazi
Indians who lived in the Four Corners region of the American
Southwest between A.D. 200 and 1300. According to Pike, the
first Anasazi—called Basket Makers—were able to settle in one
place by learning to grow corn and other foods in the arid environment. Now sedentary, the Indians were able to make baskets and pottery with which to store food and water, and they
built subterranean dwellings in which to live. About A.D. 700,
the Anasazi began erecting elaborate, above-ground, multistoried warrens. During this high time in their civilization, the
Pueblos—as the Anasazi of this period are called—built three
impressive population centers at Chaco Canyon, Mesa Verde,
and Kayenta. Pike explains that during the later part of the
1200s, however, the Anasazi began to leave the region, and by
1300, they had vanished completely. Researchers speculate that
they were driven out by drought and roving bands of Shoshonean hunters. Donald G. Pike is the author of *Anasazi: Ancient
People of the Rock*, from which this selection was excerpted.

I n the plateau country of the American Southwest there
stand sandstone monuments to a people's passage, the ves-
tigial remains of a civilization that rose, flourished, and then
disappeared. The ruins of great stone cities, crouched low on

Donald G. Pike, *Anasazi: Ancient People of the Rock*, Palo Alto, CA: American West Publishing Company, 1974. Copyright © 1974 by American West Publishing Company. Reproduced by permission of Crown Publishing, a division of Random House, Inc.

the mesa tops and nestled in caves along the sheer canyon walls of this high desert region, are the mute remnants of a world that completed its life cycle centuries before European man set foot on the shores of this continent.

THE PEOPLE

Seen now it is a civilization rendered in earth tones, hued by the soft reds, ambers, rich loam browns, and bleached tans that are the natural condition in this land of wind and sun. Built with the rock and earth that lay readily at hand and hunkered close upon the rock from which they were born, the old cities have weathered well, retreating only slightly, and then only into a more harmonious union with the face of the land. They, like the earth, abide in a quiet strength, a presence that betokens an assurance of permanence, a surety of function—for they are memorials to the inventiveness of The People.

The People are gone, but their memory and the story of their passing survives in the great stone homes they built. What they called themselves we will never know, for they left no written records; like most primitive peoples, they probably chose the name which meant "The People," for such seems to be the nature of man's self-image. Surely they did not use the name by which we know them, *Anasazi* ("The Ancient Ones"), as the Navajo called them centuries later.

We know these people also by their deeds, for they were the cliff dwellers, the builders in stone, the ancient people of the rock. The great dwellings alone are sufficient testament to their achievements, but like the name, they are more mystery than solution, piquing the curiosity and tantalizing the imagination, leading to questions about the form and substance of Anasazi life. Though long dormant, they have patiently held the echoes of Anasazi life for those who would come close enough to listen.

WETHERILL AND MASON

On a bitterly cold December day in 1888, two cowboys chasing strays through the tangled canyons and mesas above the Mancos River in southwestern Colorado broke out along the rimrock to let their horses blow and get their bearings. Under leaden skies a shifting veil of light snow swayed and pulsed on the tentative currents and eddies of the wind, obscuring their view of the canyon below and adding to a growing suspicion that it was the wrong day to be outside looking for anything. But even as they rested, a decisive draft pushed between the canyon walls, sweeping the falling snow before it; to reveal what looked like a stone house—no, a whole series of stone houses—tucked back in a huge recess in the cliffs across from them.

There, alternately hidden and then haloed by the swirling snow, standing quiet and protected under the cap rock in the natural amphitheater that eons of seeping water had carved out of the cliff face, was a complex of rooms and towers bound together in a single mass of shaped and fitted sandstone that rose, curved, dipped, and squared with a grace and delicacy that seemed to mask its sheer bulk. The two men had heard talk from their Ute neighbors that there were Indian relics to be found on the mesa, but they were not prepared for anything like this.

They made their way down the steep ravine on improvised ladders and up the broken talus slope to stand at the foot of their discovery. Small windows stared vacantly past them as they probed along the front of the buildings and scuffed the dust of undisturbed centuries. Inside, they found clay pots, a stone axe, several skeletons, and sundry discards of a hasty departure; but taken altogether, they could not be sure of what they had found. All they really knew was that a people of considerable accomplishment had lived here once—and had vanished.

What Richard Wetherill and Charlie Mason found that December day was just one of many prehistoric Indian ruins that dot the Mesa Verde, all long abandoned. Their discovery was not the first sighting of a cliff dwelling in Mesa Verde, for as early as 1874 William H. Jackson, the famed photographer of the Hayden Survey, had photographed a ruin in Mancos Canyon. But Wetherill and Mason had found Cliff Palace, the glittering jewel of Mesa Verde, preserved and protected from the erosion of time by its cave. With the subsequent discoveries of Spruce Tree House, Square Tower House, and the scores of other ruins nested in the canyon walls, it rapidly became obvious that here had been the home of a large and highly developed civilization, now gone and apparently forgotten.

The Anasazi were builders and settlers on a large and permanent scale, and it is for this that they are best remembered. At a time many centuries before the European discovery and settlement of the Americas, the Anasazi had developed a complex civilization of large and closely related communities. They erected massive and multistoried apartment buildings, walled cities, and cliff dwellings of shaped and mortared sandstone.

They were dedicated farmers who planted, tilled, and even irrigated their crops, putting by the harvest to see them through the year. They were creative craftsmen of pottery and jewelry, and practiced a highly formalized religion in distinctive ceremonial chambers. The permanence and stability that they saw in their lives was reflected in the homes they built, but for reasons not yet completely understood their civilization lacked the durability of their building. The Anasazi abandoned their homeland, leaving the great stone cities and familiar farmlands for other areas of the Southwest, eventually to mix in the amalgam of modern Pueblo.

THE FOUR CORNERS REGION

The lifeway that was Anasazi began in what we know today as the Four Corners region—where the states of Utah, Colorado, New Mexico, and Arizona come together at a common point. It is high plateau country stretching in all directions across a broken and rolling landscape that rises with abrupt sandstone mesas jaggedly carved by the deep-cutting Colorado, Little Colorado, and San Juan rivers. The southern reaches of the plateau, down into west central New Mexico and east central Arizona, are dotted with the extensive lava flows and cinder deposits of volcanic activity.

Moisture is not abundant on the plateau, and with the exception of the large, permanent rivers, the areas where it collects are chiefly a result of altitude. Moisture-bearing clouds come from the southwest, borne on winds from the Gulf of California, and are pushed up to precipitate by the high mountains and mesas. There the water forms seasonal streams or seeps through the porous sandstone to collect and form tiny springs.

This pattern of precipitation has dictated in large measure the kinds of vegetation to be found on the plateau. Along the lower elevations, where water is generally more scarce, sagebrush and juniper are found to prevail, while the better-watered land above 6,000 feet might tend toward piñon and pine. A particular area favored by peculiar circumstances of moisture or temperature will break the pattern, creating a small concentration of normally high-altitude flora such as Douglas fir at an unlikely low altitude.

The same conditions of precipitation that dictate plant life also have a profound effect on man. Water is probably the single most important commodity in the arid and semi-arid Southwest, and the earliest Indian settlers clustered close around rivers, springs, and high plateaus that promised enough water to nurture their crops.

The Anasazi found their water and built their civilization near the center of the plateau immediately surrounding the Four Corners, within the drainage basin of the San Juan River. In this region the Anasazi concentrated into three distinct and vigorous population centers at Chaco Canyon, Mesa Verde, and Kayenta. While Anasazi peoples would in time spread across the entire plateau, and the influence of their culture would reach out to affect the lives of almost every other prehistoric Indian civilization in the Southwest, these cities would remain the most striking examples of what it meant to be Anasazi.

THE GREAT POPULATION CENTERS

At Chaco Canyon, southeast of Four Corners, Anasazi reached great heights first. In the broad, long alluvial valley carved and deposited by the north fork of the Chaco Wash, they built Pueblo Bonito—eight hundred rooms covering more than three acres, reaching four and five stories high in places, nestled close against the sheer cliffs of the canyon wall but entirely free-standing. All along the canyon floor stand the ruins of other sizable pueblos, most no more than a twenty-minute trot apart, hinting at a loosely related city-state that numbered its population in the many thousands.

North and east of the Four Corners is Mesa Verde, where the art of building in the caves that sculpt the walls of the myriad canyons reached its highest levels. Originally the Anasazi of the Mesa Verde built freestanding pueblos in the open, but it is the cliff dwellings—built near the end of the Anasazi occupation of Mesa Verde—that provide the most inspiring spectacle for visitors. Preserved from the elements by the protective shelter of the caves, the cliff dwellings have survived the centuries largely intact. Above the cliffs, on the expanses between the canyons that inspired an early Spaniard of uncertain identity to name the region "Green Table," the Anasazi planted and tended their fields.

Among the rugged canyons and twisted ridges that rise toward Navajo Mountain in the southwest quadrant of the Four Corners is the Kayenta region, where Tsegi Canyon is probably typical of their architectural achievement. In Tsegi Canyon the builders worked their craft both in the caves, as at Betatakin, and in the open, as at Keet Seel, where cave dwellings and free-standing structures existed almost side by side. For reasons not precisely clear, the masons of Kayenta never reached the excellence in execution that marks the work of their kinsmen to the north and east.

For many years it was assumed by a number of archaeologists that the origins of the Anasazi were to be found in the Cochise Culture that preceded the other civilizations of southwestern prehistory, but this was difficult to prove because of a dearth of hard evidence. As a result, a hopeful blank space was left at the beginning of Anasazi chronologies, indicating that something must have been there. In the past several decades, conscientious digging has shown that the Anasazi did indeed grow from a Cochise root.

The Anasazi tradition itself can be divided into two parts: the earlier Basket Maker and the later Pueblo. The Basket Makers have been traced back in the San Juan region to about the time of Christ. They were so named, logically enough, because of the fine basketry they produced and because they had none of the pottery researchers had found in other, chronologically later archaeological sites. Many of the early Basket Makers lived in caves, although in some areas they began to build pithouses, a trend that would grow and spread. The pithouses were shallow, saucerlike dwellings, walled and roofed with a combination of logs and mud mortar. Until about A.D. 500 the Basket Makers moved within the San Juan region, dividing their time between hunting and cultivating a yellow flint corn.

FROM BASKET MAKERS TO PUEBLOS

About the year 500 changes began to appear in the Basket Maker pattern of life. The modifications were not abrupt but evolutionary and varied in time from place to place throughout the San Juan, but generally speaking, the mood of change was upon the Basket Makers about this time. In the broadest terms, they were becoming more sedentary; a greater dependence on agriculture was developing; pithouses were deepened and more permanently constructed to accommodate domestic activities and family ceremonies; and they began to build the circular, subterranean ceremonial structures that would become rigidly formalized as great kivas. They also began to make pottery, a skill apparently learned from neighbors to the south.

Toward the end of this period, nearing A.D. 700, they began to show signs of a dramatic cultural advancement. The bow and arrow made its appearance, displacing the less efficient atlatl and spear. Cotton weaving was introduced, and full-grooved axes suddenly were in use. All were signs of contact with other peoples, but the rapid acceptance of the new ways indicated that the Anasazi had an adaptable, inquisitive, and thoroughly dynamic culture.

The accomplishments of the Basket Maker Anasazi were extraordinary, but about A.D. 700 they began a transition in building techniques that earned them a new name, Pueblo, and changed the architectural modes of their Southwest neighbors. The Pueblo Anasazi built in stone and masonry, rising up to build on the surface and reserving subterranean structures for ceremonial purposes. Rapidly developing their skills as masons, the Anasazi first built a few contiguous rooms and later elaborated the style into multistoried warrens of rooms and plazas that served as cities.

Whatever the stimulus for all the change and growth, whether it came from within or without, the Anasazi multiplied the refinements in their cultural pattern dramatically during the ensuing centuries. Between about 900 and 1100, they began building some of their most impressive dwellings, raised pottery craftsmanship and decoration to hitherto unknown levels, indulged in a variety of craft arts, devoted a compelling amount of energy to religion and the construction of enormous kivas, and saw their influence spread across the entire Southwest, with certain tendrils of their culture reaching as far as southwest Texas and Nevada. Their culture spread almost intact into the Upper Rio Grande region and with slight modifications poured down over the Mogollon Rim to the mountains and deserts of central and southern Arizona to become the Sinagua and later Salado.

THE EXODUS

For two hundred years following this phenomenal florescence, the Anasazi consolidated their gains and settled down to enjoy the good life they had wrought. From roughly A.D. 1100 to 1300, the largest Pueblos were built, pottery in its most advanced forms was crafted, and the Anasazi lifeway seemed established. Some might argue that it had ceased to grow and that a culture which does not grow must necessarily begin to die. The question is largely moot, though, because before 1300 the Anasazi began to leave their homes—in some cases a full century before that date—until by 1300 the once great cities of the plateau were silent and vacant, drying in the Southwest winds like the husk of some long dead insect, retaining form but lacking the essence of a once active life.

Two plausible explanations exist for the Anasazi departure from a homeland where life was full and complete: either life had ceased to be good and they were starved out, or they were driven out by someone else. There are strong indications that a severe drought extended over the plateau from 1276 to 1299, and quite possibly the Anasazi found agriculture as they had come to depend on it impossible. There are subtle inconsistencies to the theory, however, that tend to impeach its universality, giving rise to the second possibility. Wandering Shoshonean hunters—raiders by nature—had begun to roam the plateau somewhat earlier, and given the fortresslike quality of most Anasazi pueblos and cliff dwellings, it seems possible that these raiders had begun to make part, or most, of their living by preying on the vulnerable fields of the agriculturists. If this was the case, the Anasazi would in time be forced out. Whatever the answer, and it may be a combination of both, the Anasazi departed to other regions.

Where they all went cannot be determined absolutely, but certainly some decamped to the upper and middle Rio Grande region, and others possibly formed or joined the pueblos at Ácoma, Laguna, Hopi, and Zuñi. Whatever their destinations, in the process of moving and of mixing with other peoples, the purity and vitality of the culture that had been Anasazi was seriously eroded. . . .

The life cycle of Anasazi is a remarkable documentary of a people learning to cope with the world as they found it. In little more than thirteen centuries a people walked the long road from small bands of hunters and gatherers to great communities of farms and cities. From beginning to end they took the best and the worst that nature had to dish out, and they managed not only to survive, but also to grow and prosper. They were a people who borrowed the ideas, tools, and techniques of some, and in turn lent them to others. They learned the ways to a higher civilization and then embellished on those new ways themselves. Theirs is a story of success and of failure, of challenge, ingenuity, accomplishment, and even mystery and contradiction. It is, then, a very human story—of a people who left their ghosts among the rocks.

A.D. 900 to 1512: First Contact

CHAPTER 2

LEIF ERIKSSON LANDS ON CAPE COD

THE GREENLAND SAGA

The Greenland Saga—a story about Norse adventurers and kings—was copied down by priests in the latter part of the fourteenth century. According to the old saga, Leif Eriksson became excited by Bjarni Herjolfsson's report of his discovery of a land to the southwest of Greenland. Bjarni is credited with being the first European to see America, but he was singularly incurious and did not set foot on any of the lands he saw during his voyage. Leif was of a different makeup, however, and decided to sail Bjarni's route in reverse, exploring what lands he discovered. Leif sailed from his home in Greenland in 1002, journeying south along the coast of Newfoundland and Nova Scotia to Cape Cod.

The saga explains how Leif and his men set up camp on Cape Cod, a land with moderate climate containing large quantities of salmon, grapes, and timber. Because Leif actually landed on the continent that Bjarni had merely seen, history has bestowed upon him the honor of being the first European to set foot on American soil.

There was now much talk about voyages of discovery. Leif, son of Eirik the Red of Brattahlid, went to see Bjarni Herjolfsson [who is credited with being the first European to see North America], bought his ship from him, and found her a crew, so that they were thirty-five all told. Leif invited Eirik his father to lead this expedition too, but Eirik begged off rather, reckoning he was now getting on in years, and was less able to stand

The Greenland Saga, *North American Discovery, Circa 1000–1612*, edited by David B. Quinn, Columbia: University of South Carolina Press, 1971.

the rigours of bad times at sea than he used to be. . . . Leif rode on to the ship and his comrades with him, thirty-five of them all told. There was a German on the expedition named Tyrkir.

THE JOURNEY TO CAPE COD

They now prepared their ship and sailed out to sea [from Greenland] once they were ready, and they lighted on that land first which Bjarni and his people had lighted on last. They sailed to land there, cast anchor and put off a boat, then went ashore, and could see no grass there. The background was all great glaciers, and right up to the glaciers from the sea as it were a single slab of rock. The land impressed them as barren and useless. "At least," said Leif, "it has not happened to us as to Bjarni over this land, that we failed to get ourselves ashore. I shall now give the land a name, and call it Helluland, Flatstone Land [which many believe is present-day Flat Rock Point, on the east coast of Newfoundland]." After which they returned to the ship.

After that they sailed out to sea and lighted on another land. This time too they sailed to land, cast anchor, then put off a boat and went ashore. The country was flat and covered with forest, with extensive white sands wherever they went, and shelving gently to the sea. "This land," said Leif, "shall be given a name in accordance with its nature, and be called Markland, Wood Land [Nova Scotia]." After which they got back down to the ship as fast as they could.

From there they now sailed out to sea with a north-east wind and were at sea two days before catching sight of land. They sailed to land, reaching an island which lay north of it [Nantucket Island, south of Cape Cod], where they went ashore and looked about them in fine weather, and found that there was dew on the grass, whereupon it happened to them that they set their hands to the dew, then carried it to their mouths, and thought they had never known anything so sweet as that was. After which they returned to their ship and sailed into the sound which lay between the island and the cape projecting north from the land itself. They made headway west round the cape. There were big shallows there at low water; their ship went aground, and it was a long way to get sight of the sea from the ship. But they were so curious to get ashore they had no mind to wait for the tide to rise under their ship, but went hurrying off to land where a river flowed out of a lake. Then, as soon as the tide rose under their ship, they took their boat, rowed back to her, and brought her up into the river, and so to the lake, where they cast anchor, carried their skin sleeping-bags off board, and built themselves booths. Later they decided to winter there [Cape Cod] and built a big house.

THE CAMP AT CAPE COD

There was no lack of salmon in river or lake, and salmon bigger than they had ever seen before. The nature of the land was so choice, it seemed to them that none of the cattle would require fodder for the winter. No frost came during the winter, and the grass was hardly withered. Day and night were of a more equal length there than in Greenland or Iceland. On the shortest day of winter the sun was visible in the middle of the afternoon as well as at breakfast time.

Once they had finished their house-building, Leif made an announcement to his comrades. "I intend to have our company divided now in two, and get the land explored. Half our band shall remain here at the hall, and the other half reconnoitre the countryside—yet go no further than they can get back home in the evening, and not get separated." So for a while that is what they did, Leif going off with them or remaining in camp by turns. Leif was big and strong, of striking appearance, shrewd, and in every respect a temperate, fair-dealing man.

One evening it turned out that a man of their company was missing. This was Tyrkir the German. Leif was greatly put out by this, for Tyrkir had lived a long while with him and his father, and had shown great affection for Leif as a child. He gave his shipmates the rough edge of his tongue, then turned out to go and look for him, taking a dozen men with him. But when they had got only a short way from the hall there was Tyrkir coming to meet them. His welcome was a joyous one. Leif could see at once that his foster-father was in fine fettle. He was a man with a bulging forehead, rolling eyes, and an insignificant little face, short and not much to look at, but handy at all sorts of crafts.

"Why are you so late, foster-father," Leif asked him, "and parted this way from your companions?"

By way of a start Tyrkir held forth a long while in German, rolling his eyes all ways, and pulling faces. They had no notion what he was talking about. Then after a while he spoke in Norse. "I went no great way further than you, yet I have a real novelty to report. I have found vines and grapes."

"Is that the truth, foster-father?" Leif asked.

"Of course it's the truth," he replied. "I was born where wine and grapes are no rarity."

They slept overnight, then in the morning Leif made this announcement to his crew. "We now have two jobs to get on with, and on alternate days must gather grapes or cut vines and fell timber, so as to provide a cargo of such things for my ship." They acted upon these orders, and report has it that their towboat was filled with grapes [?raisins]. A full ship's cargo was cut, and in the spring they made ready and sailed away. Leif gave the land a name in accordance with the good things they found in it, calling it Vinland, Wineland; after which they sailed out to sea and had a good wind till they sighted Greenland and the mountains under the glaciers.

THE AMERICAN INDIANS LOSE THEIR CONTINENT

Hans Koning

Hans Koning is a journalist, novelist, and author of several history books, including *The Conquest of America: How the Indian Nations Lost Their Continent*, from which the following selection was taken. Koning claims that over 100 million people lived in the Americas at the time Columbus "discovered" the "New World." In spite of that fact, European invaders justified taking land from the Indians by falsely portraying the New World as newly settled and sparsely populated wilderness. According to Koning, while the Spanish conquistadors viewed the Indians as slaves, the English colonists saw them as hindrances. The European subjugation of the Indians was aided by the Indians' lack of resistance to European diseases and their want of technological advancement in the making of weapons and other tools of war.

The Europeans who came to the Americas, either to get rich and then go home or to settle here for a new life, haven't been gracious visitors. They took over the land at all possible speed. In the process, they enslaved or killed most of the original Americans.

It is a testimony to the amazing tenacity of the human spirit amidst disaster that millions of native Americans—Indians, as we have come to call them—are surviving as Indians today. In the United States their number, from an all-time low of perhaps 300,000 around the year 1900, has risen again to 2 million.

THOSE WHO WERE HERE BEFORE

Historians used to tell us that maybe 10 million people were living in all of the Americas before the year 1492. In what is now the United States and Canada, a million hunters and nomads were supposed to have roamed the plains and forests. Until about fifty years ago, this was the generally accepted wisdom.

We now know that this estimate was totally mistaken. Anthropologists, agrarian sociologists, and many other scholars have gone over the continent acre by acre, back through history. They measured the farmland and calculated how many people it could have fed. They studied ruins of Indian towns, irrigation canals, graveyards, tax documents from the 1400s. The longer they worked, the larger the population figures became. Now we have a figure of 10 million people just for Canada and the United States. For Mexico, the estimate is now 20 to 30 million people. And the total figure for Latin America ranges from a low of 65 million to a high of more than 100 million—both figures higher than the entire population of Europe at the time. We also know that the first inhabitants of the Americas came from Asia thousands of years earlier than scholars once believed. Of course, the fewer Indians had lived here and the shorter the time they had been here, the easier it had been to see the Conquest as just one more wave in the ebb and flow of populations throughout history. But this was not an empty wilderness, or a newly settled continent. It was a densely populated land area, with many large towns. How could such a place have been "discovered" by Europeans?

NORTH AND SOUTH OF THE BORDER

When writing of the Americas, I use modern geographical names. It would be too hard on the reader to do otherwise. But we must be aware of the fact that the continent's streams, mountains, and lakes had been named before any white person had seen them. The poet who described Daniel Boone "as bestowing names on streams and founts, on plants and places yet anonymous" (the year was 1813) was painting out the Indians, turning them into non-people.

America itself was named after an early sixteenth century Italian traveler named Amerigo Vespucci. No Indian living here had an image of the whole hemisphere, so it had no name; and therefore you could argue that this was a legitimate naming. We can call ourselves lucky: compared with the *conquistadores* (the Spanish invaders and conquerors), Amerigo was an enlightened man, and one of the first scientific navigators.

THE TRADEWINDS

The tradewinds that blow across the Atlantic Ocean follow a steady pattern. Summer and winter, one set of winds blows steadily from the northeast, starting at the Tropic of Cancer, a circle around the earth at 23 1/2° northern latitude, and dying out near the equator. North of the Tropic, another set of winds blows from the American coast to Europe, where they bend south. (Latitude is the distance in degrees to the equator. From the north or south pole to the equator is 90°.)

The east and west winds form a flattened circle. The east winds blew Christopher Columbus, Amerigo Vespucci, and all who came after them from Spain and Portugal to the West Indies. The westerlies blew them home. But that same circle of winds kept the first English, French and Dutch ships away from the West Indies. Once they knew there was land out there, they got to the North American coast, but much farther north and with much greater effort, tacking up against the west winds. This pattern of invisible air currents had a dramatic effect on the fates of these two parts of the continent, north and south.

The circle of latitude that runs through the city of Dallas, Texas (32 1/2° north), more or less follows the great divide created by the ocean winds. Below that line, America was invaded and conquered by the Spaniards (except for Brazil, which fell to the Portuguese.) In the early years those invaders were mostly soldiers of fortune, assorted penniless *hidalgos* (self-styled gentlemen, too proud to do manual work), and a few priests. Their main idea was to collect gold and take it back home. Above the dividing line, the Conquest was largely the work of colonizers from Britain, Ireland, and northern Europe, men and women who left their homes for good and who became independent farmers and merchants.

From the beginning the Spaniards saw the native Americans as natural slaves, beasts of burden, part of the loot. When working them to death was more economical than treating them somewhat humanely, they worked them to death. The English, on the other hand, had no use for the native peoples. They saw them as devil worshippers, savages who were beyond salvation by the church, and exterminating them increasingly became accepted policy.

THE GAP OF AGES

If so many millions of people lived in the Americas before the Europeans arrived, how were they so quickly subjugated by so few invaders? The answer to this question has several parts.

There was, first of all, the fact that the Indian nations, like those of Europe at the time, were often divided among themselves. The Europeans were able to use one tribe or nation as an ally in the fight against another tribe or nation, until it had served its purpose and could in turn be treated as the enemy.

Another strike against the Indians was their lack of resistance to European diseases. It is now generally assumed that this continent was amazingly healthy, probably because domestic animals and cattle were rare or nonexistent. But this made the native Americans deadly vulnerable to European smallpox, tuberculosis, and other diseases. They were swept away by the thousands because they had not built up immunities to these diseases. Smallpox, for instance, played a major role in the final defeat of the Aztecs by Hernando Cortés.

But the root cause of the Indian downfall was the time gap, a gap of thousands of years of technological development which separated the west coast of Europe from the east coast of America. Just as one modern infantry battalion or a couple of tanks would wipe out all of Napoleon's armies, so the Spaniards with their armor and the Englishmen with their muskets could wipe out whole Indian nations without suffering a single casualty. In many regions, American Indian agriculture was ahead of European agriculture. In many regions there was a high civilization of art, architecture, and thought. But nowhere had the technology of war reached even the level of the ancient Assyrians, with their horses, chariots, and bronze or iron knives and swords. The Indians, north or south, had no iron or steel, no armor, no gunpowder, no horses, no attack dogs. They fought back, often for years. But by the merciless laws of physics and the science of war, they had to lose in the end.

THE VOYAGES OF CHRISTOPHER COLUMBUS

JUSTIN WINSOR

Born in 1451 in Genoa, Italy, Christopher Columbus eventually became a sailor obsessed with the idea of finding a more direct route to India. He believed that it would be faster to get to Asia by sailing across the Atlantic rather than rounding the tip of Africa. Columbus approached the king and queen of Spain with his idea. Eventually, Ferdinand and Isabella signed an agreement called the Capitulations, which granted Columbus the title of governor of any lands he discovered and the right to 10 percent of whatever riches he obtained. On August 3, 1492, Columbus embarked on his journey.

In the following selection, Justin Winsor describes how Columbus and his crew spotted land during the evening of October 11, 1492. The Spaniards landed on a small island in the Bahamas and eventually founded the first European colony in the Americas on the island they named Hispaniola, which is present-day Haiti and the Dominican Republic. Columbus returned to Spain in January 1493, and after being given various titles and honors by the king and queen, sailed back to the Caribbean on September 25, 1493. Upon his return, Columbus discovered that his colony had disappeared, so he set about establishing a new one. According to Winsor, in March 1496, Columbus was forced to return to Spain in order to defend himself against charges that he was running the colony poorly. The Spanish accepted his defense and sponsored a third voy-

Justin Winsor, *Narrative and Critical History of America*, Cambridge, MA: Houghton, Mifflin, and Company, 1886.

age. During this trip, which began in May 1498, Columbus became the first European to set foot in South America. When Columbus eventually made his way to the Spanish colony, he was arrested by the new governor and sent back to Spain in chains in October 1500. Appalled by Columbus's degradation, Ferdinand and Isabella agreed to finance the explorer's fourth voyage to the Americas. During Columbus's 1502 explorations, his ships began to leak and he was forced to land on Santo Domingo, from which he was finally rescued and shipped back to Spain in September 1504. Rich, but ill, Columbus died in Spain on May 20, 1506. Justin Winsor was a librarian at Harvard University and corresponding secretary to the Massachusetts Historical Society.

Out of the harbor of Palos [in Spain], on the 3d of August, 1492, Columbus sailed with his three little vessels. The "Santa Maria," which carried his flag, was the only one of the three which had a deck, while the other two, the "Niña" and the "Pinta," were open caravels. The two Pinzons commanded these smaller ships,—Martin Alonzo [Pinzon] the "Pinta," and Vicente [Yañez Pinzon] the "Niña."

The voyage was uneventful, except that the expectancy of all quickened the eye, which sometimes saw over-much, and poised the mind, which was alert with hope and fear. It has been pointed out how a westerly course from Palos would have discouraged Columbus with head and variable winds. Running down to the Canaries . . . , a westerly course thence would bring him within the continuous easterly trade-winds, whose favoring influence would inspirit his men,—as, indeed, was the case. Columbus, however, was very glad on the 22d of September to experience a west wind, just to convince his crew it was possible to have, now and then, the direction of it favorable to their return. He had proceeded, as he thought, some two hundred miles farther than the longitude in which he had conjectured Cipango to be, when the urging of Martin Alonzo Pinzon, and the flight of birds indicating land to be nearer in the southwest, induced him to change his course in that direction.

DISCOVERING THE NEW WORLD

About midnight between the 11th and 12th of October, Columbus on the lookout thought he saw a light moving in the darkness. He called a companion, and the two in counsel agreed that it was so. At about two o'clock, the moon then shining, a mariner on the "Pinta" discerned unmistakably a low sandy shore. In the morning a landing was made, and, with prayer and ceremony, possession was taken of the new-found island in the name of the Spanish sovereigns.

On the third day (October 14) Columbus lifted anchor, and for ten days sailed among the minor islands of the archipelago; but struck the Cuban coast on the 28th. Here the "Pinta," without orders from the Admiral, went off to seek some gold-field, of which Martin Alonzo Pinzon, its commander, fancied he had got some intimation from the natives. Pinzon returned bootless; but Columbus was painfully conscious of the mutinous spirit of his lieutenant. The little fleet next found Hayti [Haiti] (Hispaniæ insula, as he called it), and on its northern side the Admiral's ship was wrecked. Out of her timbers Columbus built a fort on the shore, called it "La Navidad," and put into it a garrison under Diego de Arana.

THE RETURN TO SPAIN

With the rest of his company and in his two smaller vessels, on the 4th of January, 1493, Columbus started on his return to Spain. He ran northerly to the latitude of his destination, and then steered due east. He experienced severe weather, but reached the Azores safely; and then, passing on, entered the Tagus and had an interview with the Portuguese King. Leaving Lisbon on the 13th, he reached Palos on the 15th of March, after an absence of over seven months.

He was received by the people of the little seaport with acclamations and wonder; and, despatching a messenger to the Spanish Court at Barcelona, he proceeded to Seville to await the commands of the monarchs. He was soon bidden to hasten to them; and with the triumph of more than a conqueror, and preceded by the bedizened Indians whom he had brought with him, he entered the city and stood in the presence of the sovereigns. He was commanded to sit before them, and to tell the story of his discovery. This he did with conscious pride. . . .

The expectation which had sustained Columbus in his voyage, and which he thought his discoveries had confirmed, was that he had reached the western parts of India or Asia; and the new islands were accordingly everywhere spoken of as the West Indies, or the New World.

The ruling Pope, Alexander VI., was a native Valencian; and to him an appeal was now made for a Bull, confirming to Spain and Portugal respective fields for discovery. This was issued May 4, 1493, fixing a line, on the thither side of which Spain was to be master; and on the hither side, Portugal. This was traced at a meridian one hundred leagues west of the Azores and Cape de Verde Islands, which were assumed to be in the same longitude practically. The thought of future complications from the running of this line to the antipodes does not seem to have alarmed either Pope or sovereigns; but troubles on the Atlantic side were soon to arise, to be promptly compounded by a convention at Torde-sillas, which agreed (June 4, ratified June 7, 1494) to move the meridian line to a point three hundred and seventy leagues west of the Cape de Verde Islands,—still without dream of the des-tined disputes respecting divisions on the other side of the globe.

THE SECOND VOYAGE

Thus everything favored Columbus in the preparations for a second voyage, which was to conduct a colony to the newly dis-covered lands. Twelve hundred souls were embarked on sev-enteen vessels, and among them persons of consideration and name in subsequent history,—Diego, the Admiral's brother, Bernal Diaz del Castillo, Alonso de Ojeda, and Juan de La Cosa, with the Pope's own vicar, a Benedictine named Buil, or Boil. Columbus and the destined colonists sailed from Cadiz on the 25th of September. The ships sighted an island on the 3d of No-vember, and continuing their course among the Caribbee [Car-ibbean] Islands, they finally reached La Navidad, and found it a waste. It was necessary, however, to make a beginning some-where; and a little to the east of the ruined fort they landed their supplies and began the laying out of a city, which they called Is-abella. Expeditions were sent inland to find gold. The explorers reported success. Twelve of the ships were sent home with In-dians who had been seized; and these ships were further laden with products of the soil which had been gathered. Columbus himself went with four hundred men to begin work at the inte-rior mines; but the natives, upon whom he had counted for la-bor, had begun to fear enslavement for this purpose, and kept aloof. So mining did not flourish. Disease, too, was working evil. Columbus himself had been prostrated; but he was able to conduct three caravels westward, when he discovered Jamaica. On this expedition he made up his mind that Cuba was a part of the Asiatic main, and somewhat unadvisedly forced his men to sign a paper declaring their own belief to the same purport.

Returning to his colony, the Admiral found that all was not going well. He had not himself inspired confidence as a governor, and his fame as an explorer was fast being eclipsed by his misfortunes as a ruler. Some of his colonists, accompanied by the papal vicar, had seized ships and set sail for home. The natives, emboldened by the cruelties practised upon them, were laying siege to his fortified posts. As an offset, however, his brother Bartholomew had arrived from Spain with three store-ships; and later came Antonio de Torres with four other ships, which in due time were sent back to carry some samples of gold and a cargo of natives to be sold as slaves. The vessels had brought tidings of the charges preferred at Court against the Admiral, and his brother Diego was sent back with the ships to answer these charges in the Admiral's behalf. Unfortunately Diego was not a man of strong character, and his advocacy was not of the best.

In March (1495) Columbus conducted an expedition into the interior to subdue and hold tributary the native population. It was cruelly done, as the world looks upon such transactions to-day.

In October 1500, Columbus was arrested and sent back to Spain in chains.

BACK IN SPAIN

Meanwhile in Spain reiteration of charges was beginning to shake the confidence of his sovereigns; and Juan Aguado, a friend of Columbus, was sent to investigate. He reached Isabella in October,—Diego, the Admiral's brother, accompanying him. Aguado did not find affairs reassuring; and when he returned to Spain with his report in March (1496), Columbus thought it best to go too, and to make his excuses or explanations in person. They reached Cadiz in June, just as Niño was sailing with three caravels to the new colony.

Ferdinand and Isabella received him kindly, gave him new honors, and promised him other outfits. Enthusiasm, however, had died out, and delays took place. The reports of the returning ships did not correspond with the pictures of Marco Polo, and the new-found world was thought to be a very poor India after all. Most people were of this mind; though Columbus was not disheartened, and the public treasury was readily opened for a third voyage.

THE THIRD VOYAGE

Coronel sailed early in 1498 with two ships, and Columbus followed with six, embarking at San Lucas on the 30th of May. He now discovered Trinidad (July 31), which he named either from its three peaks, or from the Holy Trinity; struck the northern coast of South America, and skirted what was later known as the Pearl coast, going as far as the Island of Margarita. He wondered at the roaring fresh waters which the Orinoco pours into the Gulf of Pearls, as he called it, and he half believed that its exuberant tide came from the terrestrial paradise. He touched the southern coast of Hayti on the 30th of August. Here already his colonists had established a fortified post, and founded the town of Santo Domingo. His brother Bartholomew had ruled energetically during the Admiral's absence, but he had not prevented a revolt, which was headed by Francisco de Roldan. Columbus on his arrival found the insurgents still defiant, but was able after a while to reconcile them, and he even succeeded in attaching Roldan warmly to his interests.

AGAIN TO SPAIN, THIS TIME IN IRONS

Columbus' absence from Spain, however, left his good name without sponsors; and to satisfy detractors, a new commissioner was sent over with enlarged powers, even with authority to supersede Columbus in general command, if necessary. This emissary was Francisco de Bobadilla, who arrived at Santo Domingo with two caravels on the 23d of August, 1500, finding Diego in command, his brother the Admiral being absent. An issue was at once made. Diego refused to accede to the commissioner's orders till Columbus returned to judge the case himself; so Bobadilla assumed charge of the Crown property violently, took possession of the Admiral's house, and when Columbus returned, he with his brother was arrested and put in irons. In this condition the prisoners were placed on shipboard, and sailed for Spain. The captain of the ship offered to remove the manacles; but Columbus would not permit it, being determined to land in Spain bound as he was; and so he did. The effect of his degradation was to his advantage; sovereigns and people were shocked at the sight; and Ferdinand and Isabella hastened to make amends by receiving him with renewed favor. It was soon apparent that everything reasonable would be granted him by the monarchs, and that he could have all he might wish, short of receiving a new lease of power in the islands, which the sovereigns were determined to see pacified at least before Columbus should again assume government of them. . . . He proposed a new voyage; and getting the royal countenance for this scheme, he was supplied with four vessels of from fifty to seventy tons each,—the "Capitana," the "Santiago de Palos," the "Gallego," and the "Vizcaino." He sailed from Cadiz May 9, 1502, accompanied by his brother Bartholomew and his son Fernando. The vessels reached San Domingo June 29.

THE FOURTH VOYAGE

Bobadilla, whose rule of a year and a half had been an unhappy one, had given place to Nicholás de Ovando; and the fleet which brought the new governor,—with Alonso Castillo Maldonado, Bartoloméw de Las Casas, and others,—now lay in the harbor waiting to receive Bobadilla for the return voyage. Columbus had been instructed to avoid Hispaniola; but now that one of his vessels leaked, and he needed to make repairs, he sent a boat ashore, asking permission to enter the harbor. He was refused, though a storm was impending. He sheltered his vessels as best he could, and rode out the gale. The fleet which had on board Bobadilla and Roldan, with their ill-gotten gains, was wrecked, and these enemies of Columbus were drowned. The Admiral found a small harbor where he could make his repairs; and then, July 14, sailed westward to find, as he supposed, the richer portions of India in exchange for the barbarous outlying districts which others had appropriated to themselves. He went on through calm and storm, giving names to islands,—which later explorers re-named, and spread thereby confusion on the early maps. He began to find more intelligence in the natives of these islands than those of Cuba had betrayed, and got intimations of lands still farther west, where copper and gold were in abundance. An old Indian made them a rough map of the main shore. Columbus took him on board, and proceeding onward a landing was made on the coast of Honduras August 14. Three days later the explorers landed again fifteen leagues farther east, and took possession of the country for Spain. Still east they went; and, in gratitude for safety after a long storm, they named a cape which they rounded Gracias á Dios,—a name still preserved at the point where the coast of Honduras begins to trend southward. Columbus was now lying ill on his bed, placed on deck, and was half the time in revery. Still the vessels coasted south. They lost a boat's crew in getting water at one place; and tarrying near the mouth of the Rio San Juan, they thought they got from the signs of the natives intelligence of a rich and populous country over the mountains inland, where the men wore clothes and bore weapons of steel, and the women were decked with corals and pearls. These stories were reassuring; but the exorcising incantations of the natives were quite otherwise for the superstitious among the Spaniards.

They were now on the shores of Costa Rica, where the coast trends southeast; and both the rich foliage and the gold plate on the necks of the savages enchanted the explorers. They went on towards the source of this wealth, as they fancied. The natives began to show some signs of repulsion; but a few hawk's-bells beguiled them, and gold plates were received in exchange for the trinkets. The vessels were now within the southernmost loop of the shore, and a bit of stone wall seemed to the Spaniards a token of civilization. The natives called a town hereabouts Veragua,—whence, years after, the descendants of Columbus borrowed the ducal title of his line. In this region Columbus dallied, not suspecting how thin the strip of country was which separated him from the great ocean whose farther waves washed his desired India. Then, still pursuing the coast, which now turned to the northeast, he reached Porto Bello, as we call it, where he found houses and orchards. Tracking the Gulf side of the

Panama isthmus, he encountered storms that forced him into harbors, which continued to disclose the richness of the country.

THE ABORTED COLONY

It became now apparent that they had reached the farthest spot of Bastidas' exploring, who had, in 1501, sailed westward along the northern coast of South America. Amid something like mutinous cries from the sailors, Columbus was fain to turn back to the neighborhood of Veragua, where the gold was; but on arriving there, the seas, lately so fair, were tumultuous, and the Spaniards were obliged to repeat the gospel of Saint John to keep a water-spout, which they saw, from coming their way,— so Fernando says in his Life of the Admiral. They finally made a harbor at the mouth of the River Belen, and began to traffic with the natives, who proved very cautious and evasive when inquiries were made respecting gold-mines. Bartholomew explored the neighboring Veragua River in armed boats, and met the chief of the region, with retainers, in a fleet of canoes. Gold and trinkets were exchanged, as usual, both here and later on the Admiral's deck. Again Bartholomew led another expedition, and getting the direction—a purposely false one, as it proved— from the chief in his own village, he went to a mountain, near the abode of an enemy of the chief, and found gold,—scant, however, in quantity compared with that of the crafty chief's own fields. The inducements were sufficient, however, as Columbus thought, to found a colony; but before he got ready to leave it, he suspected the neighboring chief was planning offensive operations. An expedition was accordingly sent to seize the chief, and he was captured in his own village; and so suddenly that his own people could not protect him. The craft of the savage, however, stood him in good stead; and while one of the Spaniards was conveying him down the river in a boat, he jumped overboard and disappeared, only to reappear, a few days later, in leading an attack on the Spanish camp. In this the Indians were repulsed; but it was the beginning of a kind of lurking warfare that disheartened the Spaniards. Meanwhile Columbus, with the ship, was outside the harbor's bar buffeting the gales. The rest of the prisoners who had been taken with the chief were confined in his forecastle. By concerted action some of them got out and jumped overboard, while those not so fortunate killed themselves. As soon as the storm was over, Columbus withdrew the colonists and sailed away. He abandoned one worm-eaten caravel at Porto Bello, and, reaching Jamaica, beached two others.

A year of disappointment, grief, and want followed. Columbus clung to his wrecked vessels. His crew alternately mutinied at his side, and roved about the island. Ovando, at Hispaniola, heard of his straits, but only tardily and scantily relieved him. The discontented were finally humbled; and some ships, despatched by the Admiral's agent in Santo Domingo, at last reached him, and brought him and his companions to that place, where Ovando received him with ostentatious kindness, lodging him in his house till Columbus departed for Spain, Sept. 12, 1504.

On the 7th of November the Admiral reached the harbor of San Lucas. Weakness and disease later kept him in bed in Seville, and to his letters of appeal the King paid little attention. He finally recovered sufficiently to go to the Court at Segovia, in May, 1505; but Ferdinand—Isabella had died Nov. 26, 1504—gave him scant courtesy. With a fatalistic iteration, which had been his error in life, Columbus insisted still on the rights which a better skill in governing might have saved for him; and Ferdinand, with a dread of continued maladministration, as constantly evaded the issue. While still hope was deferred, the infirmities of age and a life of hardships brought Columbus to his end; and on Ascension Day, the 20th of May, 1506, he died, with his son Diego and a few devoted friends by his bedside.

The character of Columbus is not difficult to discern. If his mental and moral equipoise had been as true, and his judgment as clear, as his spirit was lofty and impressive, he could have controlled the actions of men as readily as he subjected their imaginations to his will, and more than one brilliant opportunity for a record befitting a ruler of men would not have been lost. The world always admires constancy and zeal; but when it is fed, not by well-rounded performance, but by self-satisfaction and self-interest, and tarnished by deceit, we lament where we would approve. Columbus' imagination was eager, and unfortunately ungovernable. It led him to a great discovery, which he was not seeking for; and he was far enough right to make his error more emphatic. He is certainly not alone among the great men of the world's regard who have some of the attributes of the small and mean.

SIGHTING LAND

CHRISTOPHER COLUMBUS

Christopher Columbus gave the journal of his first voyage to the Spanish king and queen upon his return to Spain in 1493. The sovereigns never returned the original manuscript to Columbus, but they made a copy for him. Columbus's grandson later tried to get this copy of the journal published, but the project never materialized, and the copy was lost. The only surviving copy of the journal is an abstract written by Dominican historian Bartolomé de las Casas, who has been criticized by several historians for adding his own thoughts to those of Columbus.

In the journal's entry dated Thursday, October 11, 1492, Columbus describes how he and his crew first sighted land after their journey over the Atlantic Ocean. Writing in the third person, Columbus gives himself credit for being the first to see a light and surmising that land must be near. The crew landed on a small island in the Bahamas, which Columbus immediately claimed for the Spanish crown. In the journal entry, the Spanish explorer describes the native people as docile and generous and predicts that they will be easy to convert to Christianity.

H e [Christopher Columbus] navigated to the west-southwest; they had a rougher sea than they had experienced during the whole voyage. They saw petrels and a green reed near the ship. Those in the caravel *Pinta* saw a cane and a stick, and they secured another small stick, carved, as it appeared, with iron, and a piece of cane, and other vegetation which grows on land, and a small board. Those in the caravel *Niña* also saw other indications of land and a stick loaded with barnacles. At these signs, all breathed again and rejoiced. On this day, to sunset, they went twenty-seven leagues. After sunset, he steered his former course to the west; they made twelve miles an hour, and up to two hours before midnight they had made ninety miles, which are twenty-two leagues and a half. And since the caravel *Pinta* was swifter and went ahead of the admiral, she found land and made the signals which the admiral had commanded. This land was first sighted by a sailor called Rodrigo de Triana, although the admiral, at ten o'clock in the night, being on the sterncastle, saw a light. It was, however, so obscured that he would not affirm that it was land, but called Pero Gutierrez, butler of the King's dais, and told him that there seemed to be a light, and that he should watch for it. He did so, and saw it. He said the same also to Rodrigo Sanchez de Segovia, whom the King and Queen had sent in the fleet as *veedor* [a comptroller], and he saw nothing since he was not in a position from which it could be seen. After the admiral had so spoken, it was seen once or twice, and it was like a small wax candle, which was raised and lowered. Few thought that this was an indication of land, but the admiral was certain that they were near land. Accordingly, when they had said the *Salve*, which all sailors are accustomed to say and chant in their manner, and when they had all been gathered together, the admiral asked and urged them to keep a good look out from the forecastle and to watch carefully for land, and to him who should say first that he saw land, he would give at once a silk doublet apart from the other rewards which the Sovereigns had promised, which were ten thousand maravedis annually to him who first sighted it. Two hours after midnight land appeared, at a distance of about two leagues from them. They took in all sail, remaining with the mainsail, which is the great sail without bonnets, and kept jogging, waiting for day, a Friday, on which they reached a small island of the Lucayos, which is called in the language of the Indians "Guanahaní." Immediately they saw naked people, and the admiral went ashore in the armed boat, and Martin Alonso Pinzón and Vicente Yañez, his brother, who was captain of the *Niña*. The admiral brought out the royal standard, and the captains went with two banners of the Green Cross, which the admiral flew on all the ships as a flag, with an F and a Y [for Spanish King Ferdinand and Queen Isabella], and over each letter their crown, one being on one side of the ✠ and the other on the other. When they had landed, they saw very green trees and much water and fruit of various kinds. The admiral called the two captains and the others who had

In October 1492, Columbus and his near-dead crew sighted land and landed in the Bahamas.

landed, and Rodrigo de Escobedo, secretary of the whole fleet, and Rodrigo Sanchez de Segovia, and said that they should bear witness and testimony how he, before them all, took possession of the island, as in fact he did, for the King and Queen, his Sovereigns, making the declarations which are required, as is contained more at length in the testimonies which were there made in writing. Soon many people of the island gathered there. What follows are the actual words of the admiral, in his book of his first voyage and discovery of these Indies.

THE DECLARATIONS

"I," he says, "in order that they might feel great amity towards us, because I knew that they were a people to be delivered and converted to our holy faith rather by love than by force, gave to some among them some red caps and some glass beads, which they hung round their necks, and many other things of little value. At this they were greatly pleased and became so entirely our friends that it was a wonder to see. Afterwards they came swimming to the ships' boats, where we were, and brought us parrots and cotton thread in balls, and spears and many other things, and we exchanged for them other things, such as small glass beads and hawks' bells, which we gave to them. In fact, they took all and gave all, such as they had, with good will, but it seemed to me that they were a people very deficient in everything. They all go naked as their mothers bore them, and the women also, although I saw only one very young girl. And all those whom I did see were youths, so that I did not see one who was over thirty years of age; they were very well built, with very handsome bodies and very good faces. Their hair is coarse almost like the hairs of a horse's tail, and short; they wear their hair down over their eyebrows, except for a few strands behind, which they wear long and never cut. Some of them are painted black, and they are the colour of the people of the Canaries, neither black nor white, and some of them are painted white and some red and some in any colour that they find. Some of them paint their faces, some their whole bodies, some only the eyes, and some only the nose. They do not bear arms or know them, for I showed to them swords and they took them by the blade and cut themselves through ignorance. They have no iron. Their spears are certain reeds, without iron, and some of these have a fish tooth at the end, while others are pointed in various ways. They are all generally fairly tall, good looking and well proportioned. I saw some who bore marks of wounds on their bodies, and I made signs to them to ask how this came about, and they indicated to me that people came from other islands, which are near, and wished to capture them, and they defended themselves. And I believed and still believe that they come here from the mainland to take them for slaves. They should be good servants and of quick intelligence, since I see that they very soon say all that is said to them, and I believe that they would easily be made Christians, for it appeared to me that they had no creed. Our Lord willing, at the time of my departure I will bring back six of them to Your Highnesses, that they may learn to talk. I saw no beast of any kind in this island, except parrots." All these are the words of the admiral.

THE REAL STORY OF CHRISTOPHER COLUMBUS

WILLIAM BIGELOW

In the fifteenth century, Europeans sailed difficult and dangerous trade routes to India and China in order to obtain spices
and other riches. Obsessed with finding an easier way to Asia,
Italian sailor Christopher Columbus convinced the Spanish
crown to finance a journey directly west over the Atlantic
Ocean. Instead of finding a new route to India, however,
Columbus discovered that an enormous landmass stood in the
way between Europe and Asia. Columbus eventually made
four voyages to the Americas, during which time he set up a
Spanish colony and explored the regions around South and
Central America.

   In the following viewpoint, William Bigelow claims that although U.S. textbooks credit Columbus with "discovering" the
New World, in actuality the land had already been discovered,
explored, and populated by those whom Columbus named "Indians." Columbus enslaved the indigenous people by making
them search for gold or forcibly removing them to Spain where
they were sold into servitude. During the two years that Columbus governed Hispaniola (Haiti and the Dominican Republic),
one half of the entire native population was killed or killed
themselves. William Bigelow teaches at Jefferson High School
in Portland, Oregon.

William Bigelow, "Rereading the Past," *Confronting Columbus: An Anthology*, edited by
John Yewell, Chris Dodge, and Jan DeSirey, Jefferson, NC: McFarland & Company, Inc.,
1992. Copyright © 1989 by the National Council of Teachers of English. Reproduced by
permission.

M ost of my students have trouble with the idea that a book—especially a *textbook*—can lie. When I tell them that I want them to argue with, not just read, the printed word they're not sure what I mean. That's why I start my U.S. history class by stealing a student's purse.

LIES ON A GRAND SCALE

As the year opens, my students may not know when the Civil War was fought, what James Madison or Frederick Douglass did or where the Underground Railroad went, but they do know that a brave fellow named Christopher Columbus discovered America. Okay, the Vikings may have actually *discovered* America, but students know it was Columbus who mapped it and *did* something with the place. Indeed, this bit of historical lore may be the only knowledge class members share in common.

What students don't know is that year after year their textbooks have, by omission or otherwise, lied to them on a grand scale. Some students learned that Columbus sailed on three ships and that his sailors worried whether they would ever see land again. Others know from readings and teachers that when the Admiral landed he was greeted by naked, reddish skinned people whom he called Indians. And still others may know Columbus gave these people little trinkets and returned to Spain with a few of the Indians to show King Ferdinand and Queen Isabella.

All this is true. What is also true is that Columbus took hundreds of Indian slaves and sent them back to Spain where most of them were sold and subsequently died. What is also true is that in his quest for gold Columbus had the hands cut off any Indian who did not return with his or her three month quota. And what is also true is that on one island alone, Hispaniola [Haiti and the Dominican Republic], an entire race of people were wiped off the face of the earth in a mere 40 years of Spanish administration.

DISCOVERY OR THEFT?

So I begin class by stealing a student's purse. I announce that the purse is mine, obviously, because look who has it. Most students are fair-minded. They saw me take the purse off the desk so they protest: "That's not yours, it's Nikki's. You took it, we saw you." I brush these objections aside and reiterate that it is, too, mine and to prove it I'll show all the things I have inside.

I unzip the bag and remove a brush or a comb, maybe a pair of dark glasses. A tube of lipstick works best: "This is my lipstick," I say. "There, that proves it *is* my purse." They do not buy it and, in fact, are mildly outraged that I would pry into someone's possessions with such utter disregard for her privacy. (I've alerted the student to the demonstration before the class, but no one else knows that.)

It's time to move on: "Ok, if it's Nikki's purse, how do you know? Why are you all so positive it's not my purse?" Different answers: We saw you take it; that's her lipstick, we know you don't wear lipstick; there is stuff in there with her name on it. To get the point across, I even offer to help in their effort to prove Nikki's possession: "If we had a test on the contents of the purse who would do better, Nikki or I?" "Whose labor earned the money that bought the things in the purse, mine or Nikki's?" Obvious questions, obvious answers.

I make one last try to keep Nikki's purse: "What if I said I *discovered* this purse, then would it be mine?" A little laughter is my reward, but I don't get any takers; they still think the purse is rightfully Nikki's.

"So," I ask, "Why do we say that Columbus discovered America?" Now they begin to see what I've been leading up to. I ask a series of rhetorical questions which implicitly make the link between Nikki's purse and the Indians' land: Were there people on the land before Columbus arrived? Who had been on the land longer, Columbus or the Indians? Who knew the land better? Who had put their labor into making the land produce? The students see where I'm going—it would be hard not to. "And yet," I continue, "What is the first thing that Columbus did when he arrived in the New World?" Right: he took possession of it. After all, he had discovered the place.

We talk about phrases other than "discovery" that textbooks could use to describe what Columbus did. Students start with the phrases they used to describe what I did to Nikki's purse: He stole it; he took it; he ripped it off. And others: He invaded it; he conquered it.

I want students to see that the word "discovery" is loaded. The word itself carries with it a perspective, a bias; it takes sides. "Discovery" is the phrase of the supposed discoverers. It's the conquerors, the invaders, masking their theft. And when the word gets repeated in textbooks those textbooks become, in the phrase of one historian, "the propaganda of the winners."

GREED AND CRUELTY

To prepare students to examine critically the textbooks of their past we begin with some alternative, and rather un-sentimental, explorations of Columbus's "enterprise," as he called it. The Admiral-to-be was not sailing for mere adventure and to prove the world was round, as my fourth grade teacher had informed her class, but to secure the tremendous profits that were to be made by reaching the Indies. From the beginning, Columbus's quest was wealth, both for Spain and for himself personally. He demanded a 10 percent cut of everything shipped to Spain via the western route—and not just for himself but for all his heirs in perpetuity. And he insisted he be pronounced governor of any new lands he found, a title which carried with it dictatorial powers.

Mostly I want the class to think about the human beings Columbus was to "discover"—and then destroy. I read to students from a letter Columbus wrote to Lord Raphael Sánchez, treasurer of Aragón and one of his patrons, dated March 14, 1493, during his return from the first voyage. He reports being enormously impressed by the indigenous people:

> As soon . . . as they see that they are safe and have laid aside all fear, they are very simple and honest and exceedingly liberal with all they have; none of them refusing anything he may possess when he is asked for it, but, on the contrary, inviting us to ask them. They exhibit great love toward all others in preference to themselves. They also give objects of great value for trifles, and content themselves with very little or nothing in return . . . I did not find, as some of us had expected, any cannibals among them, but, on the contrary, men of great deference and kindness.

But, on an ominous note, Columbus writes in his log, ". . . should your Majesties command it, all the inhabitants could be taken away to Castile [Spain], or made slaves on the island. With 50 men we could subjugate them all and make them do whatever we want."

I ask students if they remember from elementary school days what it was Columbus brought back with him from his travels in the New World. Together students recall that he brought back parrots, plants, some gold and a few of the people Columbus had taken to calling "Indians." This was Columbus's first expedition and it is also where most school textbook accounts of

Columbus end—conveniently. Because the enterprise of Columbus was not to bring back exotic knickknacks, but riches, preferably gold. What about his second voyage?

I read to them a passage from Hans Koning's fine book, *Columbus: His Enterprise:*

> We are now in February 1495. Time was short for sending back a good "dividend" on the supply ships getting ready for the return to Spain. Columbus therefore turned to a massive slave raid as a means for filling up these ships. The brothers [Columbus and his brothers, Bartolome and Diego] rounded up fifteen hundred Arawaks—men, women and children—and imprisoned them in pens in Isabela, guarded by men and dogs. The ships had room for no more than five hundred, and thus only the best specimens were loaded aboard. The Admiral then told the Spaniards they could help themselves from the remainder to as many slaves as they wanted. Those whom no one chose were simply kicked out of their pens. Such had been the terror of these prisoners that (in the description by Michele de Cuneo, one of the colonists) "they rushed in all directions like lunatics, women dropping and abandoning infants in the rush, running for miles without stopping, fleeing across mountains and rivers."
>
> Of the five hundred slaves, three hundred arrived alive in Spain, where they were put up for sale in Seville by Don Juan de Fonseca, the archdeacon of the town. "As naked as the day they were born," the report of this excellent churchman says, "*but with no more embarrassment than animals. . . .*"
>
> The slave trade immediately turned out to be "unprofitable, for the slaves mostly died." Columbus decided to concentrate on gold, although he writes, "Let us *in the name of the Holy Trinity* go on sending all the slaves that can be sold" [emphasis in Koning].

Certainly Columbus's fame should not be limited to the discovery of America: He also deserves credit for initiating the trans-Atlantic slave trade, albeit in the opposite direction than we're used to thinking of it.

Students and I role play a scene from Columbus's second voyage. Slavery is not producing the profit Columbus is seeking. He still believes there is gold in them thar hills and the Indians are selfishly holding out on him. Students play Columbus; I play the Indians: "Chris, we don't have any gold, honest. Can we go back to living our lives now and you can go back to wherever you came from?" I call on several students to respond to the Indians' plea. Columbus thinks the Indians are lying. How can he get his gold? Student responses range from sympathetic to ruthless: Okay, we'll go home; *please* bring us your gold; we'll lock you up in prison if you don't bring us your gold; we'll torture you if you don't fork it over, etc. After I have pleaded for awhile and the students-as-Columbus have threatened, I read aloud another passage from Koning's book describing the system Columbus arrived at for extracting gold from the Indians:

> Every man and woman, every boy or girl of 14 or older, in the province of Cibao (of the imaginary gold fields) had to collect gold for the Spaniards. As their measure, the Spaniards used . . . hawks' bells. . . . Every three months, every Indian had to bring to one of the forts a hawks' bell filled with gold dust. The chiefs had to bring in about 10 times that amount. In the other provinces of Hispaniola, 25 pounds of spun cotton took the place of gold.

> Copper tokens were manufactured, and when an Indian had brought his or her tribute to an armed post, he or she received such a token, stamped with the month, to be hung around the neck. With that they were safe for another three months while collecting more gold.

> Whoever was caught without a token was killed by having his or her hands cut off. There are old Spanish prints . . . that show this being done: The Indians stumble away, staring *with surprise* at their arm stumps pulsing out blood.

> There were no gold fields, and thus, once the Indians had handed in whatever they still had in gold ornaments, their only hope was to work all day in the streams, washing out gold dust from the pebbles. It was an impossible task, but those Indians who tried to flee into the mountains were systematically hunted down with dogs and killed, to set an example for the others to keep trying. . . .

Thus it was at this time that the mass suicides began: the Arawaks killed themselves with casaba poison.

During those two years of the administration of the brothers Columbus, an estimated one half of the entire population of Hispaniola was killed or killed themselves. The estimates run from 125,000 to 500,000.

It is important students not be shielded from the horror of what "discovery" meant to its victims. The fuller they understand the consequences of Columbus's invasion of America the better they will be equipped to critically re-examine the innocent stories their textbooks have offered through the years. The goal is not to titillate or stun, but to force the question: Why wasn't I told this before?

JOHN CABOT REACHES NEW ENGLAND

VERA BROWN HOLMES

Vera Brown Holmes explains in the following selection how naturalized English citizen John Cabot became the first Englishman to voyage to North America. According to Holmes, England was far behind Spain, France, and Portugal in maritime trading and colonization because it lacked the capital, sea power, and stability to make such enterprises possible. However, the English Crown did encourage Cabot's 1497 voyage across the Atlantic.

Cabot landed in the general region of Newfoundland, and, thinking it was China, reported to the king on his return that he had found a direct route to Asia. King Henry VII financed a second voyage, but at the conclusion of this journey—which took Cabot to New England—the English sailor was forced to admit his mistake. Cabot was virtually forgotten then, although in later years England would use his voyage as the basis for its claims to all North America. Vera Brown Holmes was a professor of history at Smith College and author of several books, including *A History of the Americas, from Discovery to Nationhood*, the source of this selection.

E ngland entered late into the race for colonial possessions, and it was not until the seventeenth century that her first permanent colony was planted on the American continent. There were many reasons for the delay. Unlike Spain, Portugal, and France, England was geographically far away from the crossroads of world trade which until late in the sixteenth century continued to be the Mediterranean area. England was even practically excluded from the nearer Baltic, as this trading area in the sixteenth century was monopolized by the Hanseatic League. As for the Atlantic, Spain under the "Catholic Kings" was mistress of the sea, and continued so until the defeat of the Spanish Armada at the close of the century. English sailors possessed little technical seamanship or the knowledge of charts and instruments that was to distinguish them later. Italians, because of their centuries of experience in the Mediterranean, were the first seamen of Europe, though Spanish and Portuguese sailors were now threatening to surpass them. The English Royal Navy, as the sixteenth century opened, was small and of little account. It was not until well into Henry VIII's reign that the fleet was transferred from its medieval base on the south coast to a headquarters in the Thames and was given the support of docks and arsenals constructed for its use. English ships were few and English sailors scarce.

LITTLE ENGLISH ACTIVITY OVERSEAS

Economically England was still a small nation of six million people and was only just beginning to struggle out of the agricultural swaddling clothes of the Middle Ages. English cities were small and English merchants comparatively few in number and not yet of the moneyed class. Wealth was still largely invested in land, and liquid capital for overseas or other adventures was consequently almost totally lacking. Spain, Portugal, and France had all struggled out of the turmoil of the fifteenth century earlier than England and secured the national unification needed to provide a conscious background of strength at home so necessary before overseas adventures could be successfully embarked upon. Even when, with the succession of Henry VII, England had finally secured a strong royal house and able rulers, the lack of a wholly clear hereditary title to the crown made it advisable for the early Tudors to use extreme caution before embarking on high adventures. Furthermore, the first Tudor, Henry VII, was a frugal man and not naturally inclined to adventures of doubtful profit. His son, Henry VIII, became immersed in controversies growing out of his marital difficulties with the Church, Parliament, and foreign powers. Edward VI and Mary were both greatly absorbed in the issues of the Protestant Revolt. In the light of these circumstances it is not strange that in the first half of the sixteenth century there was relatively little English activity overseas. The country possessed neither the capital, sea power, nor freedom from distraction at home needed for such undertakings.

The first English voyages to America, however, came in this period, and though they were not followed up at the time and were long considered of little consequence, they later acquired importance as the basis on which England founded her claims to North America. The first English discovery in America came through her connection with the spice trade and was part of the excitement that followed the news of Christopher Columbus's first voyage. Its leader, John Cabot, was a member of that Italian nation which supplied all the Atlantic nations with their ablest and most imaginative navigators. When this naturalized Venetian citizen—he was born in Genoa—settled as a merchant in England (c. 1484) and became interested in trading ventures out of London and Bristol, he continued to keep in touch with Mediterranean commerce in which he had earlier been actively engaged. Having visited Mecca, the great emporium for the exchange of eastern and western goods, he fully realized the wealth to be had from the eastern trade in spices, silks, perfumes, and gems. With the support of Henry VII, English merchants had recently forced their way into a share of the commerce and carrying trade between England and the Mediterranean. But this was a comparatively small matter. If only there were some way of tapping the rich treasure house of the East directly across the Atlantic, and one in which England could share! Cabot was a student of maps and globes and grasped the significance of the progress of Portuguese voyages along the west coast of Africa, culminating in Bartholomeu Dias's feat of 1488. In the early 1490's, however, that nation had not yet proved its point by reaching India and opening for itself a superior route to the East, though the achievement could hardly be far off. Over that trade route when opened, however, Portugal would exercise a complete monopoly. A way to the East by a western route was what was needed.

CABOT'S PIONEERING VOYAGE

Under John Cabot's encouragement and perhaps personal direction, ships from Bristol were searching the seas west of Ireland for unknown islands in 1491 and 1492. Columbus's voyage seems to have excited him greatly. Like every other intelligent person in Europe, he was familiar with the idea that the world was round and he appears to have believed that Columbus had reached the true East. Somehow in the sympathetic atmosphere of the time he managed to interest a group of Bristol merchants and with their backing secured in 1496 a royal patent entitling him "to saile to all parts, countreys, and seas of the East, of the West, and of the North, under our banners and ensignes . . . to seeke out, discover, and finde whatsoever isles, countreys, regions or provinces of the heathen and infidels . . . which before this time have bene unknowen to all Christians . . ." The crown would be entitled to one fifth of the returns, although it contributed nothing but the charter. This first English overseas ven-

Cabot and his crew members reach New England.

ture, like so many later ones, was financed by private money.

Setting out on May 2, 1497, and crossing the stormy North Atlantic in the *Matthew* of eighty tons with a crew of eighty men, John Cabot reached land in the general region of Newfoundland, southern Labrador, and Nova Scotia, possibly, there is reason to think, on a western extremity of Cape Breton. He seems optimistically to have believed, though he saw no inhabitants, that he had arrived on the coast of the realms of the Grand Khan, but north of where he wished to be. Near his landfall he erected a cross and planted the royal standard of England, alongside which he hoisted the banner of Venice to indicate his own leadership of the expedition. Within three months he was back in England, where he was received with enthusiasm and was feasted at court. The king was so pleased with his report that he rewarded some of the English sailors, ordered Cabot to be paid £10 and granted him a pension of £20 a year. On the basis of this first success, Cabot secured in the following year a second patent and more backing and was able to set out on the second voyage in May, 1498, with two ships and 300 men. This time the king advanced considerable sums towards the expenses. It was hoped that he would return with his ships laden with eastern silks, spices, and gems.

It is now thought that on this second journey Cabot first steered far to the north, along the Greenland coast and then, when stopped by icebergs, turned southward and skirted the North American mainland, passing along the shores of Labrador, Newfoundland, Nova Scotia, New England, and proceeded possibly as far south as Chesapeake Bay. From this point, we know little about Cabot. On his return to England he could only have made the disappointing report that he had not found the East but new, cold, bleak, mostly uninhabited lands from which there could be no hope of gold or profitable oriental trade. He was probably considered a failure and dropped into obscurity. The results of Cabot's work, however, were extensive and important. The individual to profit most from his enterprises was his son, Sebastian Cabot, whose facile pen enabled him in later years, after he had won a glamorous reputation in the service of Spain, to magnify the part he claimed to have taken in the first of the northern voyages and thereby gain greatly enhanced prestige. After his death, John Cabot's adopted country, England, used the two early Cabot voyages as the basis for her claims to all North America.

AMERIGO VESPUCCI AND THE NAMING OF AMERICA

EDWARD GAYLORD BOURNE

Edward Gaylord Bourne was a professor of history at Yale University and is the author of *Spain in America, 1450–1580*, from which the following selection was excerpted. Bourne contends that Amerigo Vespucci does not deserve to have the American continents named after him. According to Bourne, Vespucci's fame was generated by his letters, which detailed the events of his four voyages to the New World and were published before the accounts of Christopher Columbus's discoveries. Bourne explains that a historian of Vespucci's day, who was impressed by Vespucci's claims of greatness, wrote that the New World should be called "America" after him. In consequence, most Europeans at the time believed that Vespucci discovered America in 1497. However, the Italian sailor lied about the date of his first voyage—it actually occurred in 1499—in order to claim that he discovered the New World first.

T he voyages of the Florentine Amerigo Vespucci belong rather to the literary than to the geographical history of the New World. An acute observer of things new and strange and a clever writer, he became, through the publication of his letters in the countries beyond the Pyrenees, the principal source of information about the western Indies. In these narratives he made himself the central personality; in not one of them did he mention the name of the commander under whom he

Edward Gaylord Bourne, *Spain in America, 1450–1580*, New York: Barnes and Noble, Inc., 1962. Copyright © 1962 by Barnes and Noble, Inc. Reproduced by permission.

sailed, and consequently the impression easily gained ground that he was a discoverer. His place in the history of the discoveries is the most remarkable illustration of eternal celebrity won through a happy combination of the literary gift and self-advertisement, with the co-operation of the printing-press. . . .

VESPUCCI'S VOYAGES

Vespucci's first voyage was made in 1499 [despite the fact that he claimed it occured in 1497] under Hojeda. His second, so far as can be ascertained, was made immediately upon his return from the first (it being supposed that he did not tarry in Española, as did Hojeda) with Diego de Lepe in 1500, when the westward trend of the coast of South America below eight degrees south latitude was discovered.

Vespucci's third voyage was made with a Portuguese captain in 1501, who was despatched to explore the lands just discovered by Cabral. This expedition ran down the coast of Brazil to the thirty-second degree parallel, then veered off through the south Atlantic until the fifty-second degree was reached, the highest southern latitude attained up to this time. After a fierce storm land was discovered, which is identified with the island of South Georgia.

Vespucci's fourth voyage in 1503 was undertaken with "the intention of discovering an island in the East called Melaccha, of which it was reported that it was very rich, and that it was the mart of all the ships that navigate the Gangetic and Indian seas." This project of the king of Portugal was based on the reports brought back by Cabral from Calicut in 1501. It was, therefore, a renewed effort to carry out the original design of Christopher Columbus, which was not destined to be actually accomplished until the time of Ferdinand Magellan. The details of the history of this expedition correspond to what the historian Goes tells us of the voyage of Coelho, who went over in part the same ground as that of 1501 without, however, going beyond sixteen degrees south latitude.

Of neither of these voyages was Vespucci the initiator, but according to his own account the first expedition on the return was intrusted to his command and in the second he was a captain. His name, however, is not to be found in the contemporary Portuguese histories nor in the vast mass of documents in the archives of Portugal relating to the discoveries. If his two private letters to friends had not been published in Latin, instead of having the New World called after him, his name would have been known to us only as that of a map-maker and as the official examiner of pilots in Spain.

CREATIVE LICENSE

Turning now to the products of his pen which wrought the seeming miracle, those whose authenticity is accepted consist of a letter written to Lorenzo Piero Francesco de' Medici from Lisbon, in March or April, 1503, describing his third voyage, of 1501; and of a longer letter written equally from Lisbon, in September, 1504, to his old school friend Pietro Soderini, of Florence, at that time gonfaloniere of the republic, in which he described all four of the voyages. The original of the first or Medici letter is lost, but it was translated into Latin and published late in 1503 or early in 1504 under the title "Mundus Novus." The longer letter to Soderini was published at Florence in 1505. It dropped out of sight, and only five copies are known to be extant. A French version of it, prepared for René II., duke of Lorraine, was translated into Latin and published in 1507 as an appendix to the *Cosmographiae Introductio* of Martin Waldseemüller, a professor of geography in the College of St. Dié, in Lorraine.

These letters are full of details of the strange aspects of nature and of man in the new regions. They have a confidential and personal note, perhaps not unnatural in a private correspondence, which at times rises from self-importance to self-exaltation. In variety of matter they surpass Columbus's letters about his first voyage and relate of course to a different field of exploration. In considering their extraordinary popularity it is to be remembered that Columbus's own account of his third voyage, when he discovered the main-land of South America, was not printed till the nineteenth century; nor was any description of it printed until 1504, when one appeared in the little Venetian collection of voyages entitled *Libretto de Tutta la Navigatione de Re de Spagna de le Isole et Terreni Novamente Trovati*, translated from the manuscript of Peter Martyr's unpublished *Oceani Decas*. The matter in this *Libretto* was taken over into the *Paesi Novamente Retrovati*, a larger collection published in 1507; and Peter Martyr published his *Oceani Decas* (Decade of the Ocean) in 1511.

If it is now remembered that Vespucci dated his first voyage 1497, and that his account of it was presented to the Latin-reading world in 1507, while Peter Martyr's brief account of Columbus's voyage of 1498 did not get before the Latin-reading world till

1508, in the Latin translation of the *Paesi Novamente Retrovati*, it is perfectly clear why the fame of Vespucci as the discoverer of continental South America eclipsed that of Columbus. Nor must it be forgotten that the Latin translation of the Medici letter descriptive of equatorial South America was being read all over Europe from 1503 on, for it is to this narrative more than to the other that the greatness of Vespucci's reputation was owing. . . .

VESPUCCI VERSUS COLUMBUS

Outside of Spain Vespucci decidedly eclipsed Columbus. In the peninsula the case was different. The people among whom he lived and on whose ships he sailed knew little or nothing of him. No Portuguese translation of his letters was published until 1812, and no Spanish one until 1829. Peter Martyr just mentions his Brazilian voyages; Oviedo knows him not. Las Casas regards him as an impostor, and his view is echoed by Herrera. Hardly less severe are the moderns Muñoz and Navarrete. In Portugal, Goes, Barros, and Osorio pass him in silence, and in the nineteenth century Santarem devoted a book to exposing his pretensions.

The enormous circulation of the Medici letter under the title "Novus Mundus," etc., familiarized the European public outside of Spain with the association of Vespucci's name with the New World. Impressive, too, was his apparently clear conviction that it was a new part of the world and not simply the East Indies that had been found. In the very beginning he writes of the regions which "we found and which may be called a new world (novus mundus), since our ancestors had no knowledge of them, and the matter is most novel to all who hear of it. For it goes beyond the ideas of our ancients, most of whom said there was no continent below the equator and towards the south, or if any of them said there was one they declared it must be uninhabited for many reasons. But that this opinion is false and altogether contrary to the truth this last voyage of mine has made clear." Here was a positive, clean-cut declaration of the most striking character, very different from Columbus's enthusiastic but not altogether convincing identifications of Cipango and Cathay [China] in his first letter. . . .

GIVING VESPUCCI CREDIT

We come to the first suggestion to attach the Florentine's name to this "Mundus Novus." Martin Waldseemüller, the young professor of geography at the college in St. Dié, who published the Soderini letter or narrative of the four voyages as an appendix to his *Cosmographiae Introductio,* 1507, when he enumerated the different parts of the world, wrote: "In the sixth climate towards the south pole are situated both the farthest part of Africa recently discovered, and Zanzibar, the islands of lesser Java and Ceylon, and the fourth part of the globe which since Americus discovered it may be called Amerige—*i.e.,* Americ's land or America.". . .

A little further on, when ready to take up the parts of the world unknown to the ancients, he opens his account: "Now, indeed, as these regions are more widely explored, and another fourth part has been discovered by Americus Vesputius, as may be learned from the following letters, I do not see why any one may justly forbid it to be named Amerige—that is, Americ's Land, from Americus, the discoverer, a man of sagacious mind, or America, since both Europe and Asia derived their names from women.". . .

Around Vespucci the storms of controversy have raged for three centuries and a half, and he has suffered from them. His claims for himself have not stood the test. While he has been cleared of complicity in having his name attached to the New World, it is generally accepted that he antedated his first voyage to secure a distinction which did not belong to him, and that his narratives unduly exalt himself at the expense of others equally entitled to honor.

1513 to 1536: First Explorations

CHAPTER 3

PONCE DE LEÓN DISCOVERS FLORIDA

HERBERT E. BOLTON

In the following selection, Herbert E. Bolton tells how Spanish explorer Juan Ponce de León sailed from Haiti in 1513 in search of the fabled "Fountain of Youth" but instead discovered the southern tip of Florida. Shortly after Ponce arrived in Florida, the Indians drove him and his men back out to sea. In 1521 Ponce returned to Florida in an attempt to establish a colony, but the Indians again attacked the Spaniards, this time fatally injuring Ponce. Herbert E. Bolton, who died in 1958, was a history professor at the University of California, Berkeley, and author of several books on the Spanish borderlands, including *The Spanish Borderlands: A Chronicle of Old Florida and the Southwest*, from which this selection was excerpted.

A mong the romantic exiles at Española (Haiti and Dominican Republic) was Juan Ponce de León—John of the Lion's Paunch—who had come to the island with Christopher Columbus in 1493, as a member of the first permanent colony. In Ponce's veins flowed the bluest blood of Spain. His family could be traced back to the twelfth century.

RUMORS OF GOLD

Rumors of gold drew Ponce to Porto [Puerto] Rico (1508), which island he "pacified," after the very thorough Spanish manner, sharing the honors of valor with the famous dog, Bercerillo. This dog, according to the old historian, Herrera, "made wonderful havock among these people, and knew which of them

Herbert E. Bolton, *The Spanish Borderlands: A Chronicle of Old Florida and the Southwest*, New Haven, CT: Yale University Press, 1921.

were in war and which in peace, like a man; for which reason the Indians were more afraid of ten Spaniards with the dog, than of one hundred without him, and therefore he had one share and a half of all that was taken allowed him, as was done to one that carried a crossbow, as well in gold as slaves and other things, which his master received. Very extraordinary things were reported of this dog."

Ponce was made Governor of Porto Rico, but was almost immediately removed, as the appointment had been made over the head of Don Diego Columbus, Governor of Española. Thus dispossessed of office, Ponce sought fame, and wealth, and perpetual youth, perhaps, in exploration. "It is true," writes Herrera, the royal chronicler, "that besides the principal aim of Juan Ponce de León in the expedition which he undertook, which was to discover new lands, . . . another was to seek the fountain of Bimini and a certain river of Florida. It was said and believed by the Indians of Cuba and Española that by bathing in the river or the fountain, old men became youths." What more was needed to fire the blood of an adventurer like Ponce, who already possessed influence and a fortune? Nothing, as the event proved. By means of his friends he obtained a patent from King Charles (1512), later Emperor Charles V, authorizing him to seek and govern the island of Bimini, which rumor placed to the northwest.

What Ponce hoped to accomplish in the enterprise, and also the aims of his brother conquerors, can be gathered from his patent. If Ponce was an explorer and adventurer, he, like the others, hoped also to be a colonizer, a transplanter of Spanish people and of Spanish civilization. Whoever fails to understand this, fails to understand the patriotic aim of the Spanish pioneers in America. The Catholic monarchs were a thrifty pair, and they made the business of conquest pay for itself. The successes of men like Columbus and [Hernán] Cortés played into their hands. Every expedition was regarded as a good gamble. The expenses of exploration therefore were charged to the adventurer, under promise of great rewards, in titles and profits from the enterprise, if any there might be. Under these circumstances the sovereigns lost little in any case, and they might win untold returns. And so with Ponce. By the terms of his grant he was empowered to equip a fleet, at his own expense, people Bimini with Spaniards, exploit its wealth, and, as *adelantado*, govern it in the name of the sovereign. In keeping with the method already in vogue in the West Indies, the natives were to be distributed among the discoverers and settlers, that they might be protected, christianized, civilized, and, sad to say, exploited. Though the intent of this last provision in the royal patents of the day was benevolent, the practical result to the natives was usually disastrous.

LA FLORIDA

With a fleet of three vessels, on March 3, 1513, Ponce sailed from Porto Rico and anchored a month later on the coast of the northern mainland, near the mouth of the St. John's River. Here he landed, took formal possession of the "island," and named it La Florida, because of its verdant beauty and because it was discovered in the Easter season. After sailing northward for a day, Ponce turned south again. Twice in landing on the coast he and his men were set upon by the natives. On Sunday, the 8th of May, he doubled Cape Cañaveral, called by him the Cape of the Currents; and by the fifteenth he was coasting along the Florida Keys. The strain of romance in these old explorers is well illustrated by the name which Ponce, seeker of the Fountain of Youth, gave to the Florida Keys. "The Martyrs," he called them, because the high rocks, at a distance, looked "like men who are suffering."

Ponce sailed up the western shore of the peninsula, perhaps as far north as Pensacola Bay, before he again turned southward, still unaware that Florida was not an island. Anchored off the southern end of Florida, he allowed himself to fall into a snare set for him by natives. These natives told an interesting story. There was nearby, they said, a cacique [Indian Leader] named Carlos whose land fairly sprouted gold. While Ponce and his officers were drinking in the splendid tale, the Indians were massing canoes for an attack on the Spanish ships. Two battles followed before the painted warriors were driven off and the Spaniards sailed homeward without either a sight of gold or a taste of the magic spring. But his voyage was not fruitless, for on the way back to Española Ponce made a valuable find. He discovered the Bahama Channel, which later became the route for treasure ships returning to Spain from the West Indies. It was to protect this channel that Florida eventually had to be colonized.

A SEVEN-YEAR DELAY

Ponce proceeded at once to Spain, where he "went about like a person of importance, because his qualities merited it." From the King he received another patent (1514) authorizing him to colonize not only "Bimini," which one of his ships was said to have discovered, but the "Island of Florida" as well. Just now, however, renewed complaints came in of terrible devastations wrought upon Spanish colonies by the Caribs of the Lesser Antilles. Ponce was put in command of a fleet to subdue these ferocious savages, and his plans for Florida were delayed seven years.

Meanwhile other expeditions from the West Indies found Florida to be part of the mainland. By 1519, indeed, the entire coast of the Gulf between Yucatán and Florida had been explored and charted, thus ending the Spanish hope of finding there a strait leading westward to India. Chief among these explorers of the Gulf was the good pilot Alonso Alvarez de Pineda, agent of the governor of Jamaica. He mapped the coast of Amichel—as the Spaniards called the Texas coast—and was the one to discover the mouth of that large river flowing into the Gulf which he named the Espíritu Santo, but which we know today as the Mississippi. This was twenty-two years before Hernando De Soto crossed the Father of Waters near Memphis, Tennessee. Amichel was a wondrous land, indeed, according to the reports dispatched to Spain by Pineda's master. It had gold in plenty and two distinct native races, giants and pygmies.

PONCE'S ABORTED COLONY

At last Ponce returned to his task. On February 10, 1521, at Porto Rico, he wrote to King Charles: "Among my services I discovered at my own cost and charge, the Island of Florida and others in its district . . . and now I return to that Island, if it please God's will, to settle it." According to Herrera, the rare old chronicler, it was emulation of the conqueror of Mexico that aroused Ponce to make this venture. For now "the name of Hernando Cortés was on everybody's lips and his fame was great." In February, then, Ponce again set sail, with two ships, two hundred men, fifty horses, a number of other domestic animals, and farm implements to cultivate the soil. By the King's command, monks and priests accompanied him for missionary work among the natives.

Ponce landed on the Florida coast, probably in the neighborhood of Charlotte Harbor, where, on his earlier voyage, the natives had regaled him with fables of the golden realm of Carlos, the cacique, and had attacked his ships. Since then slave-hunting raids along their coast had filled these warlike, freedom-loving

Florida natives with an intense hatred for Spanish invaders. Hardly had the colonists begun to build houses when the Indians set upon them with fury. The valiant Ponce, leading his men in a counter attack, received an Indian arrow in his body. Some of his followers were killed. This disaster put an end to the enterprise. Ponce and his colonists departed and made port at Cuba, having lost a ship on the way. A few days later Ponce died from his wounds, leaving unsolved the mystery of the Fountain of Youth. Over his grave in Porto Rico, where his body was sent for burial, his epitaph was thus inscribed:

Here rest the bones of a LION,
Mightier in deeds than in name.

So perished the discoverer and first foreign ruler of Florida, as many another standard-bearer of the white race on this soil was to perish, from the dart of the irreconcilable Indian.

THE TEMPLE MOUND BUILDERS

ROY S. DICKENS JR.

Roy S. Dickens Jr. is director of the Research Laboratories of Anthropology at the University of North Carolina at Chapel Hill. In the following selection, Dickens describes the advanced civilization that flourished in the American southeast between A.D. 1100 and 1600. He explains that the first Spanish explorers to the region found large religious and administrative centers ruled by powerful chiefs. Within these centers were large mounds, which served as platforms for ceremonial buildings, houses for the nobility, and mortuaries containing the remains of ranking persons and valuable objects. Unfortunately, this "Mississippian" or "Temple Mound" civilization—second only in the Americas to those in Mexico and Peru—was destroyed by the Europeans, who brought disease and disruption.

When the Spanish explorers first entered the southeastern part of North America in the sixteenth century, they found themselves in a strange "New World." They discovered that the native peoples of the Southeast, especially in the interior portions, possessed a highly complex and sophisticated culture. The conquistadors encountered large areas of political control, which they called "provincia," and social systems as intricate as those of much of contemporary Europe.

Since the explorers were searching for valuables for themselves and to enrich the royal treasury, they took special interest in the places where the Indian rulers were buried. Although the mortuary temples contained no gold or silver, there was an impressive array of sumptuary objects of engraved shell, carved wood,

Roy S. Dickens Jr., *Of Sky and Earth: Art of the Early Southeastern Indians*, Dalton, GA: Lee Printing Company, 1982. Copyright © 1982 by Lee Printing Company. Reproduced by permission of the High Museum of Art, Atlanta, Georgia.

embossed copper, polished stone, and chipped stone. These objects were used by the Indian nobles to verify their positions in life, and often the same objects were buried with them at death.

THE ROOTS OF AN ADVANCED CIVILIZATION

The Indian groups observed and described by the European explorers were descendants of people who had wandered into northwestern North America from Asia as early as about 30,000 B.C. In the Southeast, archaeological evidence of early hunting-and-gathering groups has been dated back to about 12,000 B.C. These early people lived in small nomadic bands, had no agriculture, and lacked a strongly defined leadership. Most of their technological skills were devoted to manufacturing hunting weapons and food-processing tools.

By around 3,000 B.C., the Southeastern peoples had begun to practice rudimentary horticulture and to live in seasonal villages. They also developed a concern for death and an afterlife, which is reflected in formalized burial practices. Populations grew, group territories were defined, and technologies began to manifest artistic concerns as well as functional efficiency.

In the millennia which followed, cultivated plants became increasingly important in the economy of the Southeastern Indians. Squash and gourds were among the first cultigens, with later additions of corn and beans. A stable and productive subsistence base contributed to the development of a more settled lifestyle and complex social organization. An agricultural economy also gave rise to changes in religious concepts, as the people attempted to understand, predict, and control nature. Leadership became solidly fixed in an elite class of priest-chiefs, who demanded special ritual goods and were accorded much attention at death.

By around A.D. 500–800, Southeastern culture had entered a climactic stage of development. This culture, called "Temple Mound" or "Mississippian" by archaeologists, was the one observed in all its glory by the sixteenth-century Spanish explorers. It had evolved over thousands of years to reach a level of complexity second in the Americas only to the great civilizations of Mexico [the Aztecs] and Peru [the Incas].

MISSISSIPPIAN CHIEFDOMS

Archaeological remains of the Mississippian culture are abundant in the river valleys of the Southeast. Prominent are the sites of large religious-and-administrative centers (called "ceremonial centers"), such as Etowah in northern Georgia, Moundville in central Alabama, Spiro in eastern Oklahoma, and Cahokia in west central Illinois. These sites are surrounded by numerous lesser centers and hundreds of villages and hamlets. The ceremonial centers and their satellite settlements sometimes formed sociopolitical units that anthropologists have termed "chiefdoms." A chiefdom was controlled by a single powerful hereditary ruler. One such ruler, Tascaluza, was described by Fidalgo de Elvas, a chronicler of the 1539–41 expedition of Hernando de Soto:

> The Cacique was at home, in a piazza. Before his dwelling, on a high place [a platform mound], was spread a mat for him, upon which two cushions were placed, one above the other, to which he went and sat down, his men placing themselves around, some way removed, so that an open circle was formed about him, the Indians of the highest rank being nearest to his person. One of them shaded him from the sun with a circular umbrella, spread wide, the size of a target, with a small stem, and having deer-skin extended over cross-sticks, quartered with red and white, which at a distance made it look of taffeta, the colours were so very perfect. It formed the standard of the Chief, which he carried into battle. His appearance was full of dignity: he was tall of person, muscular, lean, and symmetrical. He was the suzerain of many territories, and of a numerous people, being equally feared by his vassals and the neighbouring nations. The Field-Marshall, after he had spoken to him, advanced with his company, their steeds leaping from side to side, and at times towards the Chief, when he, with great gravity, and seemingly with indifference, now and then would raise his eyes, and look on as in contempt.

The Etowah site, near present-day Cartersville, Georgia, has many features typical of the larger Mississippian centers. Six pyramidal earthen mounds, one of which contains over four million cubic feet of earth, were positioned around a prepared-clay plaza. The mounds, plaza, and hundreds of dwellings, granaries, and other structures were surrounded by a deep ditch and massive log palisade. This site is situated on the banks of the Etowah River in an expansive valley of rich alluvial soils.

Mississippian Mounds

Mississippian mounds served as platforms for ceremonial buildings and for houses of the nobility. At least one mound at each center supported a mortuary temple (charnel house), where the remains of ranking persons were interred and where valuable mortuary paraphernalia were stored. One of these sacred buildings was described by Garcilaso de la Vega, another chronicler of the de Soto expedition:

> The ceiling of the temple, from the walls upward, was adorned like the roof outside with designs of shells interspersed with strands of pearls and seed pearls which were stretched so as to adhere to and follow the contour of the roof. Among these decorations were great headdresses of different colors of feathers such as those made for wear, and . . . both pearls and feathers seemed to have been placed in the air at different levels so that they would appear to be falling from the roof. In this manner the ceiling of the temple was adorned from the walls upward, and it was an agreeable sight to behold.
>
> Glancing now from the roof downward, our captains and soldiers perceived that along the highest of the four walls of the temple there were two rows of statues, ranged one over the other. These were figures of men and women, and were of the normal size of the people of that land, who are as large as Philistines. On the floor along the walls were some wooden benches which were excellently carved, as was everything in that temple; and resting upon these benches were the chests which served as sepulchres for the lifeless bodies of the curacas [chiefs] who had been lords of the province . . . , their children, their brothers and sisters, and their nieces and nephews, no one else being buried in that temple.

The plazas were used for public ceremonies, dances, deliberations, and games. An important annual ceremony was probably similar to the historically-documented Busk. The Busk was held over several days in late summer when the first corn had ripened. It was a "new year" rite, where grievances were settled, sins forgiven, and life begun afresh. Favorite games probably included stickball (the original lacross), and "chunkey," in which young men first rolled a stone disc and then competed at throwing sticks closest to a spot where the disc would stop rolling. Stone discoidals, thought to have been used in the game of chunkey, have been found in burials at a number of Mississippian sites.

In the 800 to 1,000 years of Mississippian cultural development, levels of power and prosperity shifted between the various Southeastern chiefdoms. The local elite, who functioned in both secular and sacred capacities, demanded food, labor, and scarce resources from their constituent populations. In return, the populace relied on their chiefs for direction in agricultural pursuits, leadership in warfare, and intercession with the spirit world. Survival of a chiefdom depended on sustained success at warfare, crop productivity, and internal social cohesion.

Mississippian societies did not survive European onslaught, which brought insurmountable disease and disruption. Some of the people and vestiges of their culture did survive, however, and these are known to us today as the Creeks, Cherokees, Choctaws, Chickasaws, Natchez, Seminoles, Yuchis, and others.

HOW RABBIT FOOLED ALLIGATOR: A CREEK LEGEND

TRADITIONAL

The Creek Indians, who lived mainly in Florida and Georgia during the first Spanish explorations to the region, enjoyed telling the following story to their children, who delighted in hearing it.

One day in the Florida Everglades, Rabbit tricked Alligator into leaving the safety of his home in the water. Rabbit provoked Alligator into wanting to prove he was brave enough to confront the Devil—who Rabbit said would be up on the hill the following day—even if it meant leaving the safety of the swamp. The next morning, the determined Alligator set off up the hill. Once the reptile was far from water, however, Rabbit set the hill on fire and laughed as Alligator burned in the flames. Alligator tumbled down the hill into the swamp and never trusted Rabbit again.

When the animals talked with each other just like people do today, a very handsome alligator lay sunning himself luxuriously on a log in which we now call the Florida Everglades. Then along came Mr. Rabbit, who said to him, "Mr. Handsome Alligator, have you ever seen the devil?"

THE TRICKSTER

"No, Mr. Rabbit, but I am not afraid of the devil. Are you?" replied Mr. Alligator.

Traditional, "How Rabbit Fooled Alligator," *Voices of the Winds: Native American Legends*, New York: Facts On File, 1989.

"Well now, Mr. A., I did see the devil. Do you know what he said about you?" asked Rabbit.

"Now, just what did the devil have to say about me?" Alligator replied.

"The devil said that you are afraid of him," said Rabbit. "Besides, he said you would not even look at him."

"Rubbish," said Alligator. "I know that I am not afraid of the devil, and I am not afraid to look at him. Please tell him so for me the next time you see him."

"I do not think you are willing to crawl up the hill the day after tomorrow and allow me to introduce you to the devil himself," said Rabbit.

"Oh, yes, I am willing and ready to go with you," replied Alligator. "Let us go tomorrow."

"That is just fine with me," replied Rabbit. "But Mr. A., when you see some smoke rising somewhere, do not be afraid. It is a sign that the devil is moving about and will soon be on his way."

"You do not have to worry about me," said Alligator. "I told you I am not afraid of the devil."

"When you see the friendly birds flying about, and the deer running at a gallop, do not be afraid," said Rabbit.

"Don't you be concerned, because I will not be afraid," repeated Alligator.

"If you hear some fire crackling and it comes closer to you, do not be scared," said Rabbit. "If the grasses near you begin to smoke, do not be scared. The devil is only wandering about. Then is the time for you to get a good look at him when the heat is hottest."

After Rabbit's final words of wisdom, he left Alligator sunning himself.

RABBIT HATCHES HIS PLAN

Next day, Rabbit returned and asked Alligator to crawl up the hill, following him. Rabbit led him to the very top and directed him to lie in the tallest grass. Then Rabbit left Alligator, laughing to himself all the way down the hill, because he had led Alligator to the farthest place away from his home in the water.

On his way, Rabbit came to a smoldering stump. He picked up a piece, carrying it back to the high grass, where he made a fire so the wind blew it toward Alligator.

Soon the fire surrounded the place, burning closer and closer to Alligator. Rabbit then ran to a sandy knoll and sat down to watch the fun, chuckling over the trick he had played on Mr. Alligator.

Only a short time passed when the smoke rose in thick spirals, and the birds flew upward and away. Other animals ran for their lives across the field.

Alligator cried out, "Oh, Mr. Rabbit, where are you?"

"You just lie there quietly," replied Rabbit. "It's only the devil prowling about."

The fire began to roar and spread rapidly. "Oh, Mr. Rabbit, what is that I hear?" asked Alligator.

"That's just the devil breathing hard," replied Rabbit. "Do not be scared. You will see him soon!"

Rabbit became so amused that he rolled and rolled on the sandy knoll and kicked his heels up in the air with glee.

Soon the grass surrounding Alligator caught fire and began to burn beneath him. Alligator rolled and twisted with pain from his burns.

"Do not be afraid now, Mr. Alligator," called Rabbit. "Just be quiet for a little while longer, and the devil will be there for you to get a firsthand look at him."

Alligator could not stand any more toasting! He started to crawl as fast as he could down the hillside toward the water. He wriggled through the burning grass, snapping his jaws, rolling in pain, and choking from the smoke.

Rabbit, upon his sandy knoll, laughed and laughed, jumping up and down with delight at the trick he had played on Alligator.

"Wait a minute, Mr. A. Don't be in such a hurry. You said you were not afraid of the devil," called Rabbit.

By that time Alligator had reached his home in the water, tumbling in to stop the pain of his roasted skin.

Never again did Mr. Handsome Alligator trust that trickster, Mr. Rabbit, or any of his family, ever!

VERRAZANO'S GREAT MISTAKE

SAMUEL ELIOT MORISON

Samuel Eliot Morison relates in the following selection how Italian sailor Giovanni Verrazano was engaged by the king of France in 1524 to locate a water route through North America to China. Verrazano explored the entire eastern coast from Florida to Newfoundland, and at North Carolina's Outer Banks he made the mistake for which he would thereafter be noted. According to Morison, Verrazano thought the narrow sand spits that parallel the coast of North Carolina were the mainland and that the water beyond the banks was the Pacific Ocean. Verrazano's error would be perpetuated for more than a century, reflected in maps that showed the North American continent tapering to a narrow isthmus around the region of Cape Fear, North Carolina. Samuel Eliot Morison was a professor of history at Harvard University and the author of several books, including *The European Discovery of America: The Northern Voyages, A.D. 500–1600*, from which this excerpt was taken.

G iovanni Verrazzano's plan for his ocean crossing ran parallel to that of Christopher Columbus in 1492; but instead of dropping down to latitude 28°N and the Canaries, he chose to take off from Las Desertas in the Madeira group at latitude 32°30'N. French corsairs had already been preying on the Spanish treasure fleets, Spanish warships were looking for prowling Frenchmen, and Verrazzano obviously wished to avoid hostile confrontations in order to carry out his mission [of discovering a passage through North America to China]. The Madeiras were Portuguese.

Samuel Eliot Morison, *The European Discovery of America: The Northern Voyages*, A.D. 500–1600, New York: Oxford University Press, 1971. Copyright © 1971 by Oxford University Press. Reproduced by permission.

FAREWELL TO THE OLD WORLD

On 17 January 1524 [Verrazzano's ship] *La Dauphine* said farewell to the Old World. The latitude the Captain chose for the crossing lay well above the normal range of easterly trade winds, but for about three weeks *La Dauphine* enjoyed them: "Sailing with a zephyr blowing east-southeast with sweet and gentle mildness," as he puts it in his Letter [to the king of France]. Like Columbus, Verrazzano appreciated the beauty of smooth seas and prosperous winds, and on the northerly edge of the trades he had them at their best.

On 24 February he ran out of luck, and encountered as sharp and severe a tempest as he or his shipmates had ever experienced. "With the divine help and merciful assistance of Almighty God and the soundness of our ship, accompanied with the good hap of her fortunate name, we were delivered," wrote Verrazzano. He altered course to west by north, and then turned west on latitude 34°N. Thus he made landfall on or about 1 March 1524 at or near Cape Fear, which is on latitude 33°50'47"N; Verrazzano said it was on 34°, "like Carthage and Damascus." Near enough—Damascus is on 33°30'. Note that this navigator, like [English sailor John] Cabot, compared latitudes of his discoveries with known points in Europe, which meant something to those who read his report.

LANDING AT CAPE FEAR

Cape Fear, southernmost of North Carolina's three capes (Fear, Lookout, and Hatteras), is a long alluvial promontory where the Cape Fear River has been depositing detritus for many millennia. The tip is formed by Bald Island, a tract of still unspoiled dunes and wet marsh where birds, fish, and turtle breed, and a live-oak forest grows, and the Frying Pan Shoals extend some fifteen miles farther out to sea. Verrazzano did not tarry, as he wished to explore the coast between there and Florida before turning northward. His distances are difficult to follow on the map, because every unit is "50 leagues" (about 110 nautical miles). . . .

So, from her landfall, *La Dauphine* sailed south for "fifty leagues," then turned north again "in order not to meet with the Spaniards." Since she had not found any "convenient harbor whereby to come a-land," the turning point must have been short of Charleston; on Girolamo da Verrazzano's [Verrazzano's brother] map this point is called *Dieppa*, after *La Dauphine's*

home port. Returning to the place of her landfall, she anchored
well off shore, probably in the lee of Cape Fear. Unlike other
mariners of the period, Verrazzano liked anchoring in an open
roadstead, provided he found good holding ground. However,
he sent a boat ashore on or near Cape Fear, and briefly con-
sorted with a group of natives who "came harde to the Sea side,
seeming to rejoyce very much at the sight of us; and, marveil-
ing greatly at our apparel, shape and whiteness, showed us by
sundry signs where we might most commodiously come a-land
with our boat, offering us also of their victuals to eat."

Verrazzano here describes their manners and customs "as
farre as we could have notice thereof":

> These people go altogether naked except only that they
> cover their privy parts with certain skins of beasts like
> unto martens, which they fasten onto a narrow girdle
> made of grass, very artificially [i.e. artfully] wrought,
> hanged about with tails of divers other beasts, which
> round about their bodies hang dangling down to their
> knees. Some of them wear garlands of birds' feathers.
> The people are of color russet, and not much unlike the
> Saracens; their hair black, thick, and not very long,
> which they tie together in a knot behind, and wear it
> like a tail. They are well featured in their limbs, of
> mean [average] stature, and commonly somewhat big-
> ger than we; broad breasted, strong arms, their legs
> and other parts of their bodies well fashioned, and they
> are disfigured in nothing, saving that they have some-
> what broad visages, and yet not all of them; for we saw
> many of them well favoured, having black and great
> eyes, with a cheerful and steady look, not strong of
> body, yet sharp-witted, nimble and great runners, as
> far as we could learn by experience; and in those two
> last qualities they are like to them of the uttermost
> parts of China.

This reference to China indicates that Verrazzano was familiar
with *The Book of Ser Marco Polo*.

Continuing some distance northward, the Frenchmen again
landed, noted sand dunes fronting the upland palmettos, and
bay bushes and cypresses "which yield most sweet savours, far
from the shore"—even a hundred leagues out. So he named this
land *Selva di Lauri* (Forest of Laurels), and *Campo di Cedri* (Field
of Cedars). Like Columbus, Verrazzano had a genius for giving

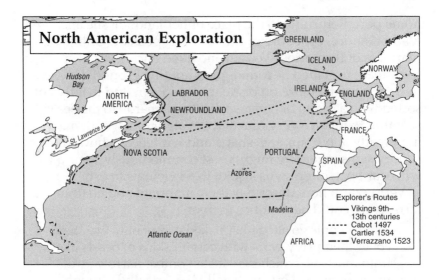

newly discovered places beautiful and appropriate names; but, unlike those given by Columbus, few of his names stuck. Unless an explorer is shortly followed by others, or by colonists of his nation, his names are quickly forgotten.

As laurel and cedar grow all along the coasts of Georgia and South Carolina, we cannot identify these places. Strange that neither the Florentine, nor the Englishmen who came here in 1585–90, mentioned the yucca palm, with its spiky fronds and great clusters of white blossoms. Possibly it did not grow that far north in the sixteenth century.

ENCOUNTER ON THE OUTER BANKS

Continuing north-northeasterly, *La Dauphine* anchored again in an open roadstead and sent a boat ashore. Here is how [nineteenth-century navigation historian Richard] Hakluyt translates Verrazzano's story of the encounter:

> While we rode on that coast, partly because it had no harbor, and for that we wanted water, we sent our boat ashore with 25 men; where, by reason of great and continual waves that beat against the shore, being an open coast without succour, none of our men could possibly go ashore without losing our boat. We saw there many people, which came unto the shore, making divers signs of friendship, and showing that they were content we should come a-land, and by trial we found them to be very courteous and gentle, as your majesty shall under-

stand by the success. To the intent we might send them
of our things, which the Indians commonly desire and
esteem, as sheets of paper, glasses, bells and such trifles,
we sent a young man, one of our mariners, ashore, who
swimming towards them, cast the things upon the
shore. Seeking afterwards to return, he was with such
violence of the waves beaten upon the shore, that he
was so bruised that he lay there almost dead, which the
Indians perceiving, ran to catch him, and drawing him
out, they carried him a little way off from the sea.

The young man, fearing to be killed, "cried out piteously," but
these Indians had no sinister intention. They laid him down at
the foot of a sand dune to dry in the sun, and beheld him "with
great admiration, marveling at the whiteness of his flesh." They
then stripped him down and "made him warm at a great fire,"
which caused his shipmates to expect him to be roasted and
eaten.

> The young man having recovered his strength, and
> having stayed awhile with them, showed them by
> signs that he was desirous to return to the ship; and
> they with great love clapping him fast about with
> many embracings, accompanying him unto the sea;
> and, to put him in more assurance, leaving him alone
> they went unto a high ground and stood there, be-
> holding him, until he was entered into the boat. This
> young man observed, as we did also, that these are of
> color inclining to black, as the other were; with their
> flesh very shining, of mean stature, handsome visage,
> and delicate limbs, and of very little strength; but of
> prompt wit. Farther we observed not.

This spot Verrazzano named *Annunziata* because the day was
25 March, the feast of the Annunciation of the Virgin. It must
have been on the Outer, or Carolina, Banks between Capes
Lookout and Hatteras, or a few miles north of Hatteras. According to his own marginal note, Verrazzano here committed
his great geographical error. He found "an isthmus a mile in
width and about 200 long, in which, from the ship, we could see
el mare orientale [the Pacific Ocean], halfway between West and
North"; i.e. northwesterly. This sea, he says, "is the same which
flows around the shores of India, China and Cataya. . . . " To this
isthmus the discoverer gave the name *Verrazzania*, and the entire land discovered was called *Francesca* after King François.

The Great Mistake

This passage has attracted a good deal of scorn to the Florentine mariner, but without justice. You may sail for twenty miles south and twenty miles north of Cape Hatteras without seeing the mainland from the deck or mast of a small sailing ship. We flew Verrazzano's route on a beautiful June day with high visibility at an altitude of two hundred feet, and for fifty miles could see no land west of the Banks. Even from the modern motor road, which (spliced out with car ferries) extends along the Banks, the far shore is commonly invisible. Verrazzano is, however, open to two criticisms. (1) In view of his preference for open roadsteads, why did he not anchor off one of the inlets and send in a boat to explore? These inlets are always shifting, but we cannot imagine that there were none in 1524, since the flow of fresh water always breaks out new ones when an old one closes. Sir Walter Raleigh's colonists found at least three in the 1580's with two fathom of water in each. (2) Verrazzano must have been familiar with a similar topography, on a smaller scale, in the Venetian lagoon; but there you can almost always see foothills from outside the Lido.

The Letter continues: "We sailed along this isthmus," i.e. the Outer Banks, "in continual hope of finding some strait or northern promontory at which the land would come to an end, in order to penetrate to *quelli felici liti del Catay*"—those happy shores of Cathay [the coast of China].

Rather pathetic, is it not? Verrazzano and his shipmates straining their eyes to find a bold, northward-looking promontory like Cape St. Vincent or Finisterre, which *La Dauphine* could whip around in a jiffy, and everyone on board would shout and yell, and the musicians would strike up the *Vexilla Regis*, knowing that they had found the long-sought Passage to India.

Thus Verrazzano assumed that he had sighted the Pacific Ocean across an isthmus much narrower than that of Panama! This tremendous error was perpetuated for a century or more by his brother Girolamo and the Italian cartographer [Vesconte] Maiollo. Their world maps give North America a narrow waist around North Carolina, with the Pacific Ocean flowing over some 40 per cent of the area of the future United States. . . .

Evaluating Verrazzano

The results of Verrazzano's voyage along the North American coast were largely negative. The "Isthmus" and "Sea" of Verrazzano, his only positive contributions, turned out to be pure fantasies—but they influenced North American cartography for over a century. By reporting the absence of any strait between Florida and Nova Scotia, he turned the exploratory efforts of France and England northward; Jacques Cartier took up the quest where Verrazzano left off, and Frobisher continued it, further north. Neither discovered "the happy shores of Cathay," but empire followed in their wakes, whilst France completely ignored that of *La Dauphine*, which subtended a land of riches immeasurable—the Carolinas, Virginia, New York, New England. But it was not Verrazzano's fault that the French government remained indifferent to the opportunities that he opened.

There is no blinking the fact that Verrazzano missed many important places, and that he was singularly incurious. His habit of avoiding harbors caused him to miss great bays such as the Chesapeake, the Delaware, and the Hudson estuary, leaving them for the English, Dutch, and Swedes to explore and colonize in the following century. His failure to take a good look at the mouth of the Hudson River is perhaps the greatest opportunity missed by any North American explorer. But no sailor will blame him for missing things, since most of them have done so themselves. The great Captain Cook missed Sydney Harbor. [Francis] Drake and all the Spanish navigators missed the Golden Gate and San Francisco Bay, which were discovered by an overland expedition. Why, even Des Barres's Royal Navy team of surveyors in 1770 missed Northeast Harbor, Maine!

Let us, however, judge Verrazzano by what he tried to do, rather than by what he accomplished. If he failed to find the strait "to the happy shores of Cathay," it was because it was not there; his attainable vision of a New France stretching from Newfoundland to Florida faded because king and country were not interested. His greatest ambition . . . had been to people the regions he discovered with French colonists, to introduce European plants and domestic animals, and to bring the "poor, rough and ignorant people" of North America to Christianity. When one contemplates the fate of the North American Indians, one cannot be very enthusiastic over these benevolent gestures of European pioneers; but at least they tried.

THE NARVÁEZ DEBACLE

IAN K. STEELE

Hoping to find gold such as Hernando Cortez had discovered in Mexico, Pánfilio de Narváez led an expedition to Florida in 1528. Historian Ian K. Steele explains that unfortunately for the Spaniards, the Florida Indians had little that the Spaniards considered valuable other than food. Furthermore, in response to Narváez's unprovoked attacks, the Indians became hostile. According to Steele, after a grueling and unsuccessful march through the Florida swamps, where the Spaniards were attacked by Indians and contracted malaria, Narváez decided to abort the expedition. After eating their horses for food and dismantling their armor for metal needed for the construction of watercraft, the Spaniards set sail for Mexico on makeshift boats. However, the boats were not seaworthy, and only four of the two hundred forty-two men who originally began the journey made it to Mexico. Ian K. Steele is a history professor at the University of Western Ontario and author of several history books, including *Warpaths: Invasions of North America*, from which this selection was excerpted.

Spanish interest in North America, like that of the rest of Europe, was revived once the astounding wealth of the Central American Aztec empire became clear. Spanish officialdom soon sought to control the fortunate renegade Hernando Cortés [who conquered Mexico City], and venturers like Pánfilio de Narváez wanted to find "other Mexicos." Narváez had become wealthy in the conquests of Hispaniola [Haiti and

Ian K. Steele, *Warpaths: Invasions of North America*, New York: Oxford University Press, 1994. Copyright © 1994 by Oxford University Press. Reproduced by permission.

the Dominican Republic], Jamaica, and Cuba, where he had gained a reputation as particularly brutal and untrustworthy. Ambitious to duplicate the success of his rival Cortés and to curb Cortés's empire on the north, Narváez launched his own major expedition. Armed with a perpetual royal grant to the entire northern Gulf coast and its unlimited hinterlands, but required by a new royal order to give fair treatment to native peoples, Narváez sailed directly from Spain in June 1527 with a force of six hundred volunteers in five ships.

A Promising Expedition

Although a third of the men deserted in the West Indies and half the horses died during passage, the expedition seemed promising enough once it reached Florida. The landing was safely beyond the territory of the Calusa [Indians], who had thwarted [Juan] Ponce de León and [Hernando de] Córdoba, and relations with the inhabitants began cautiously. An officer of the expedition was landed on an island, where he traded with the Timucua [Indians] for fish and venison. Some forty thousand Timucua, divided into two rival confederations and some fifteen distinct tribes, are thought to have lived in numerous sizable villages across north central Florida, sustained by farming, hunting, and fishing. It is not known what these particular villagers knew of the Timucuan encounter with Ponce de León fifteen years earlier, but their approach was also cautious.

What we know of the disastrous Narváez invasion of Florida comes from the memoirs of Alvar Nuñez Cabeza de Vaca, one of only four known to have survived the expedition. The day after the initial trading, Narváez landed as many men as the ship's boats could hold. They found the Timucua village, which included one dwelling that could accommodate more than three hundred people, entirely evacuated. If the Timucua had planned to encourage the Spaniards to re-embark by offering no hospitality, the plan failed, for "amid some fish nets we found a gold rattle." The next day, Narváez landed the rest of his men and the forty-two surviving horses, and ceremonially claimed the country for Charles V. The following day, some villagers approached; although there were no interpreters and little comprehension, Cabeza de Vaca was sure that "their many signs and threats left little doubt that they were bidding us to go."

A Disastrous March

After scouting, and unwisely sending his fleet to an inadequately known rendezvous farther north, Narváez marched his three hundred remaining men to Tampa Bay without discovering any of the cornfields they had presumed would be a source of provisions. The Spanish captured four Amerindians, showed them corn, and were taken to a small field of green corn near a village. These surprised Timucua offered no resistance to the invaders, even when the Franciscan commissary ordered the burning of the revered remains of their ancestors. The villagers did offer the usual refrain that whatever interested the intruders, particularly gold, could be found in abundance in the land of their rivals, in this case the powerful Apalachee to the north.

As the Spanish moved northward, they found the country without people, settlements, or food. After fifteen days on ships' rations, they saw some two hundred Timucua approaching them with what the Spanish regarded as menacing gestures. The Spanish attacked, reportedly without inflicting any casualties but again taking a few prisoners, who led them to precious edible corn and guided them on toward "Apalachen." The Spanish marched northward for another month "without seeing a native who would let us catch up to him." The Timucua could regard their strategy as successful; despite the destruction of some revered objects and the loss of some grain, the intruders had been moved along without reported loss of life on either side.

Approaching the Apalachicola River, the Spanish were met by Dulchanchellin, a chieftain accompanied by a large retinue including musicians playing reed flutes. He was carried on a man's back, which appeared ludicrous to the Spanish who equated status with horsemanship and were themselves mounted on the first horses ever seen in the area. After an hour of exchanging gifts and gestures, which may not have conveyed much more than did the mutually incomprehensible words, the Spanish believed Dulchanchellin to be an enemy of the Apalachee. He led the expedition to his village and fed them, but when they awoke, the Spaniards found themselves alone in the village.

As the Spaniards proceeded, they saw that they were being shadowed by Amerindians. Since this army was recruited in Spain rather than the Spanish Caribbean, the men wore hot, heavy breast- and back plates as well as metal helmets. The tired and hungry Spaniards, many with open wounds caused by the chafing of armor that to date seemed unnecessary, recorded relief as they reached their first major objective, the Apalachee village they called Apalachen.

A SURPRISE ATTACK

Narváez ordered an entirely unprovoked surprise attack. Ten horsemen and fifty infantry fell upon the village of forty small thatched huts nestled defensively in a clearing between lakes. The attack met no resistance, as the men were not in the village. Apalachee bowmen soon retaliated, skirmishing from the cover of nearby swamps and tall cornfields. From scouting forays and from prisoners, the Spanish learned that, though they were in the biggest village of the Apalachee, there were no riches. The only treasures had been corn, deerskins, roughly woven cloth, and corn-grinding bowls. After three weeks of sporadic fighting, resulting in the death of an Aztec prince accompanying the expedition and in the frequent wounding of armored men and horses, Narváez became increasingly interested in prisoners' reports about Aute, nine days to the southwest.

After an uneventful first day in which no inhabitants were seen, the expedition was chest deep in a lake when it was attacked by bowmen who wounded several men and horses. These unidentified warriors, likely Apalachee, harried the marching Spaniards, then disappeared when a counterattack was launched. Successes lured the warriors to challenge the Spaniards in an open area, but mounted Spanish lancers chased them off, killing two. For the next eight days, the wary Spaniards saw no one.

As the Spaniards approached Aute, near the mouth of the Apalachicola, they came under random attack. A prominent *hidalgo* was killed by an unseen adversary whose arrow found the space between helmet and body armor. The Aute, who were allies of the Apalachee, had evacuated and burned their village before the Narváez expedition arrived, though some food was found. Narváez and about a third of the Spanish infantry soon came down with malaria, and the encampment endured night attack. The cavalry plotted to desert what was now a doomed venture, but accepted a plan to build boats with which the whole expedition could escape.

Lessons learned from the military encounter with Florida bowmen are evident in the boat building. Armored horses, a ma-

jor Spanish advantage against astonished Aztec and Inca infantry, had seldom been effective in the swamps and bush of this
region, and the prized horses were now needed for food. To get
iron for boat construction, armorers reworked not only stirrups
and spurs, but also the metal-tipped arrows for the crossbows.
Spanish crossbows had failed to compete with Amerindian long-
bows that were six to seven feet long, thick as a man's arm, and
very accurate at two hundred yards. Although Spanish armor
had been effective against most arrows encountered on three
continents, these Aute arrows penetrated six inches of wood,
and even Spanish breast- and back plates. Ten Spaniards were
killed while foraging. "We found their bodies pierced all the way
through, although some of them wore good armor." Some flint
arrowheads shattered against armor, producing wounding
shards. Cabeza de Vaca's tragic story of the 250 who escaped
from this "Bay of Horses," is an extraordinary postscript to the
fourth failed Spanish invasion of Florida.[1] Only 4 of the 250 eventually made their way to Mexico City.

---

1. The three other failed invasions included those by Ponce de León, Hernando de Córdoba and Lucas Vásquez d'Ayllón.

THE BAY OF HORSES

Álvar Núñez Cabeza de Vaca

In 1527, Pánfilo de Narváez led an expedition to Florida in search of gold. During the expedition, many of the Spaniards fell ill from malaria and died during Indian attacks. Starving and exhausted, some of the men threatened to desert their captain. In August 1528, the haggard band of men arrived at a bay along the west coast of Florida and made plans to find a way home.

In the following selection, Álvar Núñez Cabeza de Vaca, a member of the Narváez expedition, recounts how the Spaniards decided to construct makeshift boats on which to sail to Mexico. However, no one had any knowledge of shipbuilding, they had no supplies with which to construct boats, and many of the men were weak with sickness and starvation. Nevertheless, against all odds, the men built five boats out of metal salvaged from their armor, fronds and sap from indigenous plants, and the hides of their horses, which they had killed for food and supplies. Thereafter, the Spaniards referred to the region as the Bay of Horses, in memory of the mounts they had killed there. Unfortunately, all but four men, including Cabeza de Vaca, perished during the arduous journey to Mexico. Cabeza de Vaca was the first European to describe America from Florida through Arizona and author of the oldest written history of Native Americans.

We left Aute [on August 3, 1528], and traveled all day before coming to the place I had visited. The journey was extremely arduous. There were not horses enough to carry the sick, who went on increasing in numbers day by day, and we knew of no cure. It was piteous and painful to witness our perplexity and distress. We saw on our arrival how small

Álvar Núñez Cabeza de Vaca, *Relation of Nuñez Cabeza de Vaca*, Ann Arbor, MI: University Microfilms, Inc., 1966.

were the means for advancing farther. There was not any where to go; and if there had been, the people were unable to move forward, the greater part being ill, and those were few who could be on duty. I cease here to relate more of this, because any one may suppose what would occur in a country so remote and malign, so destitute of all resource, whereby either to live in it or go out of it; but most certain assistance is in God, our Lord, on whom we never failed to place reliance. One thing occurred, more afflicting to us than all the rest, which was, that of the persons mounted, the greater part commenced secretly to plot, hoping to secure a better fate for themselves by abandoning the Governor [Pánfilo de Narváez] and the sick, who were in a state of weakness and prostration. But, as among them were many hidalgos [lesser-ranking members of the nobility] and persons of gentle condition, they would not permit this to go on, without informing the Governor and the officers of your Majesty [Spanish King Charles V]; and as we showed them the deformity of their purpose, and placed before them the moment when they should desert their captain, and those who were ill and feeble, and above all the disobedience to the orders of your Majesty, they determined to remain, and that whatever might happen to one should be the lot of all, without any forsaking the rest.

ONE GREAT PROJECT

After the accomplishment of this, the Governor called them all to him, and of each apart he asked advice as to what he should do to get out of a country so miserable, and seek that assistance elsewhere which could not here be found, a third part of the people being very sick, and the number increasing every hour; for we regarded it as certain that we should all become so, and could pass out of it only through death, which from its coming in such a place was to us all the more terrible. These, with many other embarrassments being considered, and entertaining many plans, we coincided in one great project, extremely difficult to put in operation, and that was to build vessels in which we might go away. This appeared impossible to every one: we knew not how to construct, nor were there tools, nor iron, nor forge, nor tow, nor resin, nor rigging; finally, no one thing of so many that are necessary, nor any man who had a knowledge of their manufacture; and, above all, there was nothing to eat, while building, for those who should labor. Reflecting on all this, we agreed to think of the subject with more deliberation, and the conversation dropped from that day, each going his way, commending our course to God, our Lord, that he would direct it as should best serve Him.

The next day it was His will, that one of the company should come saying, that he could make some pipes out of wood, which with deer-skins might be made into bellows; and, as we lived in a time when any thing that had the semblance of relief appeared well, we told him to set himself to work. We assented to the making of nails, saws, axes and other tools of which there was such need, from the stirrups, spurs, crossbows and the other things of iron there were; and we laid out for support, while the work was going on, that we would make four entries into Aute, with all the horses and men that were able to go, and that on every third day a horse should be killed to be divided among those who labored in the work of the boats and the sick. The incursions were made with the people and horses that were available, and in them were brought back as many as four hundred fanegas of maize [about six hundred forty bushels]; but these were not got without quarrels and contentions with the Indians. We caused many palmitos to be collected for the woof or covering, twisting and preparing it for use in the place of tow for the boats.

THE BUILDING OF THE BOATS

We commenced to build on [August 4], with the only carpenter in the company, and we proceeded with so great diligence that on the twentieth day of September, five boats were finished twenty-two cubits in length, each caulked with the fibre of the palmito. We pitched them with a certain resin, made from pine trees by a Greek, named Don Theodoro; from the same husk of the palmito, and from the tails and manes of the horses we made ropes and rigging, from our shirts, sails, and from the savins growing there, we made the oars that appeared to us requisite. Such was the country into which our sins had cast us, that only by very great search could we find stone for ballast and anchors, since in it all we had not seen one. We flayed the horses, taking the skin from their legs entire, and tanning them to make bottles wherein to carry water.

During this time some went gathering shell-fish in the coves and creeks of the sea, at which employment the Indians twice attacked them and killed ten men in sight of the camp, without our being able to afford succor. We found their corpses traversed from side to side with arrows; and for all some had on good armor, it did not give adequate protection or security against the nice and powerful archery of [the Indians]. According to the declaration of our pilots under oath, from the entrance to which we had given the name *Bahía de la Cruz* [Bay of the Cross] to this place, we had traveled two hundred and eighty leagues or thereabout. Over all that region we had not seen a single mountain, and had no information of any whatsoever.

Before we embarked there died more than forty men of disease and hunger, without enumerating those destroyed by the Indians. By the twenty-second of the month of September, the horses had been consumed, one only remaining; and on that day we embarked in the following order: In the boat of the Governor went forty-nine men; in another, which he gave to the Comptroller and the Commissary, went as many others; the third, he gave to Captain Alonzo del Castillo and Andrés Dorantes, with forty-eight men; and another he gave to two captains, Tellez and Peñalosa, with forty-seven men. The last was given to the Assessor and myself, with forty-nine men. After the provisions and clothes had been taken in, not over a span of the gunwales remained above water; and more than this, the boats were so crowded that we could not move: so much can necessity do, which drove us to hazard our lives in this manner, running into a turbulent sea, not a single one who went, having a knowledge of navigation.

1537 to 1542: The Second Wave of Exploration

CHAPTER 4

THE DE SOTO EXPEDITION

ROBERT J. FLYNN

In the following selection, Robert J. Flynn explains how Hernando de Soto led an expedition to what is now the southeastern United States in 1539. According to Flynn, de Soto's methods of conquest were brutal: He forcibly took Indian women as concubines for his men, extorted food from the Indians, and retaliated against Indian attacks by slaughtering any Indians he could find.

The most significant conflict that occurred between de Soto and the Indians was the battle for Mabila (or, Mavilla), an Indian trading center located in present-day Alabama. According to Flynn, between twenty-five hundred and five thousand Indians died in the battle. Overall, de Soto's expedition resulted in thousands of Indians dying in battle and tens of thousands dying as a result of diseases that the Spaniards brought with them. Many Spaniards died as well, and de Soto himself died of illness in May of 1542. De Soto's failure to find rich empires in North America caused other Spaniards to lose interest in the region for several decades. Robert J. Flynn has written about several explorers for Gale Group's American Eras history series.

R uthless Ambition. Perhaps no one better exemplified the savage nature of the sixteenth-century Europeans who invaded North America than Hernando de Soto. A captain in the Spanish army at the age of twenty, de Soto had served as Francisco Pizarro's chief military advisor during Spain's ruthless conquest of Peru in the early 1530s. While de

Soto had become a wealthy man as a result of that venture, he remained restless and desired to increase his fortune. Evidence of gold in the southeastern part of North America consequently spurred him to organize an expedition in hopes of finding another New World empire to plunder.

FOLLOWERS AND METHODS

Followers. De Soto organized his expedition in the port city of Havana on the island of Cuba. His force consisted of 330 infantrymen equipped with swords, harquebuses, and crossbows, and 270 cavalrymen armed with swords and lances. Primarily veterans of earlier New World expeditions, his men opted for the lighter and more effective Aztec armor over the heavy and ineffective European variety. His force also included about 100 slaves, servants, camp followers, and pig herders. Finally, the expedition took with it mules to carry baggage, a herd of hogs—the ancestors of today's southern razorbacks—to provide a source of food, and a pack of brutal Irish hounds to hunt and kill Indians in the swamps of the Deep South.

Methods. By using the approach pioneered by Hernando [Hernán] Cortés and Pizarro, de Soto hoped to avoid the fate that had befallen the Pánfilo de Narváez expedition a decade earlier.[1] Like his predecessors, de Soto planned to use advanced weapons, armored cavalry, and better tactics to dominate the numerically superior Indians. More important, he aimed to gain information, secure concubines for his men, ensure against attack, and extort the food on which his expedition depended by taking a tribe's leader hostage upon entering its territory. When Indians did attack, moreover, he planned to retaliate savagely by slaughtering any he could find and burning their settlements.

CONFLICTS WITH THE INDIANS

Early Campaign. Conflict with the Indians began as soon as de Soto's men landed at Tampa Bay in May 1539. Timucuan [Indian] hit-and-run attacks increased in frequency because de Soto's men ruthlessly torched settlements and mercilessly killed peaceful Indians who approached them. When the Spanish

---

1. The Pánfilo de Narváez expedition to Florida, begun in 1527, ended disasterously. Failing to find gold and deserted by supply ships, Narváez and his men built several small boats and sailed for Mexico. Unfortunately, most of the boats sank and most of the men died from drowning, starvation, disease, and Indian attacks. Only three men— including Alvar Núñez Cabeza de Vaca—made it to Mexico.

passed into Apalachee [Indian] territory they stumbled into a large, skillfully laid ambush at a difficult swamp crossing. The Apalachee thereafter constantly harassed de Soto's men—who wintered in their territory—by attacking suddenly and by ambushing small, isolated detachments. De Soto retaliated by killing any Apalachees that his men caught.

Ocute and Cofitachequi. While de Soto's relations with Native Americans were almost universally hostile, he did not war with every tribe he encountered. The Ocute of southern Georgia, in fact, allied with his expedition for an attack on their rivals, the Cofitachequi. The alliance with the Ocute was short-lived, however, and reflected the difference between European and Indian military objectives. The Ocute took vengeance on their traditional foe by killing and taking scalps in the first few Cofitachequi villages they entered. They then returned to their homeland satisfied that they had evened the score with their rivals. The Spanish, in contrast, sought wealth to plunder and food to fuel their expedition; de Soto's men consequently looted pearls and other valuables from the Cofitachequis' temples and forced the Indians to supply them with corn.

Battle of Mabila. De Soto's only major pitched battle occurred later in 1540 in the large [Indian] trading center of Mabila, located in present-day Alabama. As was their custom, the Spanish seized the Mabilan chief, Tazcaluza, upon meeting him on the outskirts of his chiefdom. Tazcaluza was ingratiating and compliant; he gladly escorted de Soto's men to Mabila, where, he promised, they would find great stores of food and many women. Unbeknownst to de Soto, though, the Mabilan chief had laid an elaborate trap designed to destroy the unsuspecting Spaniards. Shortly after de Soto's men entered the town, Tazcaluza sprang the trap by escaping from his Spanish guards. Suddenly, Indian warriors leapt from hiding, rained arrows on the invaders, and forced them out of the town with heavy casualties. Believing that they had routed de Soto, the Indians pursued the fleeing Spanish into the open fields outside Mabila's fifteen-foot palisades. The Spanish, however, were preparing a trap of their own. After luring the Native Americans away from the protection of Mabila's walls by feigning a disorderly retreat, de Soto's elite, armored cavalry suddenly spun about and launched a devastating counterattack that crushed the Indians' charge. Soon thereafter, the Spanish infantry reentered the town and set it to the torch while de Soto's powerful cavalry prevented any Indians from escaping the conflagration.

Consequences. Native American losses at Mabila were staggering. Between twenty-five hundred and five thousand had died in the battle, most burning to death in the inferno that consumed the town. The Spanish likewise suffered heavily even though they wore Aztec armor and enjoyed the overwhelming advantage of cavalry: hundreds had been injured; more than forty had died; and they had lost some three dozen horses. More important, the battle had eroded seriously the expedition's morale and had led de Soto and his lieutenants to doubt whether they could conquer and control the Indians of North America as they had the Aztec and Incan empires.

DE SOTO'S DEATH AND LEGACY

Death. Increasingly desperate because he had discovered no gold and because his men were becoming mutinous, de Soto moved northward into Chicaza [Indian] territory in hopes of finding treasure. That proved to be a poor decision, however, because the Chicaza had developed a new tactic for dealing with the Spanish invaders: night attacks. In one especially effective night assault on de Soto's winter camp, the Chicaza greatly weakened the expedition by killing a dozen Spaniards and slaughtering more than fifty horses. Continued night raids eventually drove the Spanish force westward across the Mississippi, where they destroyed many Indian villages and seized large quantities of corn. Then, while moving south along the Mississippi in the spring of 1542, de Soto suddenly took ill. He died in May and was replaced as commander by one of his lieutenants, Luis de Moscoso y Alvarado.

The End. Having heard rumors of Coronado's expedition in the southwestern part of North America, Moscoso decided to move west through the plains of Texas in hopes of joining his countrymen. His men soon ran low on provisions and began to suffer grievous losses from the Tonkawa Indians' skillfully laid ambushes. Desperate for food and weary from the Native Americans' constant harassing attacks, the Spanish returned to the Mississippi, where they spent the winter of 1542–1543. Deciding to abandon the expedition that spring, Moscoso's men constructed seven barges on which they planned to escape to Mexico. Their conflict with the Indians had not yet ended, however. A coalition of Mississippi valley tribes temporarily put aside their differences and joined together to pursue the Spanish down the river in a flotilla of canoes. Later, javelin-throwing Indians warred with the Spanish as they passed westward along the Gulf Coast. In the end, only about three hundred survivors—half the number that landed with de Soto at Tampa Bay—returned to Spanish Mexico.

Impact. De Soto's expedition had profound ramifications for all the parties involved. It demonstrated that North America lacked easily plundered treasure and that the Indians were still too powerful to conquer. Consequently Spanish authorities lost interest in La Florida for several decades. As for the Native Americans, they were able to drive the Spanish out of North America despite the invaders' superior weapons, better tactics, and irresistible armored cavalry. On the other hand, they had suffered thousands of deaths in battle and had lost tens of thousands more as a result of the diseases that the Spaniards had brought with them. De Soto's invasion thus weakened the southeastern Indians greatly and left them increasingly unable to withstand the European incursions that grew steadily during the seventeenth century.

De Soto's Destruction of Mabila

The Gentleman from Elvas

In 1540, the de Soto expedition arrived at the Indian trading center of Mabila (or, Mavilla), located in present-day Alabama. The Spanish immediately seized the Indian chief Tazcaluza to ensure the Indians' compliance, and the chief led de Soto's men into town where he promised them food and women. However, Tazcaluza had laid a trap for the Spaniards. Shortly after de Soto's men entered Mabila, the Indians attacked and forced them out of the town. Encouraged, the Indians pursued the Spaniards across an open field.

The Gentleman from Elvas, an unknown Portuguese knight who participated in de Soto's expedition, describes in the following selection how the Spanish regrouped at the outskirts of Mabila and drove the Indians back into town. De Soto's men torched buildings and shot at any Indians trying to escape the conflagration. The Gentleman from Elvas estimates that around twenty-five hundred Indians and eighteen Spaniards died in the attack. This selection is excerpted from the Gentleman from Elvas's famous narrative about the de Soto expedition entitled "Account by a Gentleman from Elvas."

As soon as the battle line and rear guard reached [the Indian trading center at] Mavilla, the governor [de Soto] ordered all those who were best armed to dismount and

The Gentleman from Elvas, *The De Soto Chronicles: The Expedition of Hernando De Soto to North America in 1539–1543*, Tuscaloosa: University of Alabama Press, 1993. Copyright © 1993 by University of Alabama Press. Reproduced by permission.

made four companies of foot. The Indians, on seeing how the governor was drawing up his men, urged the cacique [the Indian leader Tazcaluza] to leave, telling him, as was later learned from some Indian women who were captured there, that he was only one man and could fight for one only; that there were many principal men of the Indians there, very daring and skillful in matters of war, any of whom could direct all the other men; that since matters of war and victory were a hazard of fortune and there was no certainty as to which of the sides would be victorious, he should endeavor to place his person in safety, so that if they should end their lives there, as they had resolved to do rather than allow themselves to be vanquished, he would be left to govern the land. However, he refused to go, but so much did they urge him that he went out of the town with twenty or thirty of his Indians. From the clothing of the Christians he took a scarlet cloak and some other pieces—all that he could carry and which pleased him most. The governor was advised that the Indians were going out of the town, and he ordered those who were mounted to surround it. In each foot company, he ordered a soldier with a firebrand to set fire to the houses so that the Indians would have no shelter. Having arranged all his men in order, he ordered an arquebus fired. At the signal, all four companies, each in its own position, attacked with great fury and doing great damage entered the town from one side and the other. The friar and the secular priest and those who were with them in the house were rescued, which cost the life of two men of ability and courage who went thither to help them.

The Indians fought with so great spirit that they drove us outside again and again. It took them so long to get back that many of the Christians, tired out and suffering great thirst, went to get a drink at a pond located near the stockade, but it was tinged with the blood of the dead and they returned to the fight. The governor, seeing this, with those who accompanied him entered the town on horseback together with the returning foot. This gave an opportunity for the Christians to succeed in setting fire to the houses and overthrow and defeat the Indians. As the latter fled outside the town from those on foot, those on horse again drove them within the gates, where, having lost hopes of escape, they fought courageously; and after the Christians had come among them cutting with the sword, seeing that they were assailed beyond repair, many fled into the burning houses, where, piled up one on top of the other, they were suffocated and burned to death. In all, those who were killed there numbered two thousand five hundred or thereabout. Of the Christians eighteen were killed there, one of whom was Don Carlos, the governor's brother-in-law, another, his nephew, another, Juan Gamez, [and others including] Mem Rodriquez, a Portuguese, and Juan Vázquez of Villanova de Barcarota—all men of honor and pride. The others [killed] were foot soldiers. Besides those killed, one hundred and fifty Christians were wounded, receiving seven hundred arrow wounds. It was God's will that they were healed shortly of very dangerous wounds. Twelve horses were also killed and seventy wounded. All the clothing carried by the Christians, the ornaments for saying mass, and the pearls were all burned there. The Christians set fire to them; for they considered as more annoying the hurt which the Indians could do them from within the houses where everything was gathered together. The governor learned there that Francisco Maldonado was awaiting him in the port of Ochuse and that it [Ochuse] was six days' journey from there. He arranged with Juan Ortiz that he should keep still about it, so that the men might not oppose his determination, and because the pearls which he desired to send to Cuba as samples had been burned; for if the news [of the ship] were noised about the men might desire to go to that land [Cuba]. And fearing that if news were heard of him, unless they saw gold or silver, or anything of value, it [Florida] would acquire such a reputation that no man would desire to go thither when people might be needed; consequently, he determined not to give news of himself so long as he did not find a rich land.

CORONADO DISCOVERS THE SEVEN CITIES

BERNARD DEVOTO

In the following selection, Bernard DeVoto describes Francisco Vásquez de Coronado's search for the Seven Cities, which were reputed to contain many riches. DeVoto claims that the spectacular expedition to what is now the southwestern United States was comprised of more than a thousand people and at least fifteen hundred horses, mules, and beef cattle.

In the spring of 1540, Coronado and his followers reached Cíbola—one of the Seven Cities. According to DeVoto, the Spaniards were shocked. Rather than spectacular cities of gold, the Seven Cities turned out to be Zuni pueblos containing nothing the Spaniards valued except food. In spite of his disappointment, Coronado dutifully claimed the pueblos for Spain and subjugated the Indians by killing dozens of them. Coronado then resolved to find riches in other regions nearby. He sent out parties that eventually discovered the Grand Canyon, conquered the Tiwa Indian settlement in the Rio Grande valley, and found the Indian village of Quivira in present-day Kansas. Bernard DeVoto was a historian, critic, novelist, educator, conservationist, and the author of several books on American history, including *The Course of Empire*, from which this selection was excerpted.

Bernard DeVoto, *The Course of Empire*, Cambridge, MA: Houghton Mifflin Company, 1952. Copyright © 1952 by Bernard DeVoto. Reproduced by permission of the publisher.

[N ew Spain's (present-day Mexico) Viceroy Antonio de] Mendoza organized the conquest of Cíbola [one of the mythic Seven Cities reputed to be as rich as the Inca Empire] with unhurried thoroughness. Following the return of Fray Marcos [who claimed to have seen Cíbola and reported that it was as rich as the Spaniards thought], he sent a detachment of cavalry to reconnoiter the route again and fraternize with the Indians. It was led by a first-rate frontier commander, Melchior Díaz, the alcalde of Culiacán who had welcomed [Alvar Nuñez] Cabeza de Vaca [who had traveled the region after the disastrous Narváez expedition in Florida] when he arrived there; it went all the way to the Arizona desert south of the Gila River. He provided three vessels under Hernando de Alarcón, to sail up the Gulf of California, get in touch with and support the main expedition, and explore northward or wherever by sea—for Cíbola must be in or on the edge of Asia. To head the conquest, which was set for 1540, he appointed his young friend Francisco de Coronado, whom he had already made governor of New Galicia [roughly, the present-day Mexican state of Jalisco].

A MOST BRILLIANT COMPANY

Not yet thirty, well born, married to a woman of even higher station, Coronado was a soldier but had not been a conquistador. He put down an Indian revolt in his province, firmly but not vindictively—a promise of better times in New Galicia. That finished, in 1539 he was off to find another El Dorado in the Sonora mountains, east of the route Fray Marcos took. Nothing; and the mountains turned him back. Then as tidings of the rich Cíbola overspread Mexico, he was commissioned captain-general—absolute and independent head—of the whole enterprise. Fray Marcos, who had been made father provincial of the Franciscans in Mexico on Mendoza's insistence, was named to accompany him. Marcos would lead the friars of the Church spiritual and would guide Coronado, the deputy of the Church militant.

There was no dearth of recruits to conquer the Seven Cities. To a humble settler of Culiacán who joined the expedition and became its annalist, it seemed "the most brilliant company ever collected in the Indies to go in search of new lands." They were splendor when Mendoza reviewed them at Campostela, south of Culiacán, in February 1540. Two hundred and thirty caballeros, some with many horses, and sixty-two footmen were mustered in there. There were five friars with humbler assistants, a military guard, and their private Indians. (Eventually the total force reached 336.) Nearly a thousand Indians went along as servants and auxiliaries, and were a great strain on the commissary. There were at least fifteen hundred horses, mules, and beef cattle. Most of the arms were those of medieval hand-to-hand fighting, advanced technology being represented by only nineteen crossbows, seventeen arquebuses, and a few bronze popguns on wheels that were no good. Nearly everyone wore armor, though a lot of it was only leather cuirasses, or shirts of mail. Coronado, riding down the line of pennons at review, with the music playing and the trumpets like Caesar's and the gentlemen of Spain shouting to St. James, looked like El Dorado. His armor was gilded and two plumes waved from his helmet.

The expeditionary force which looked like a parade moved so slowly that on April 22 Coronado set out ahead with a light column of about one hundred. Among the optimisms of Fray Marcos had been statements that the Indian trails through the mountains were excellent roads and nearly level, and that there were food and forage all the way. It proved far otherwise and from the foothills on the troopers found the going vile. The gallant idlers of Mexico City were seasoned very soon; they gaunted on short rations, mountain slopes, and waterless marches, and so did their horses. Their bellies were concave and their eyes sunken by the time they reached the chromatic Arizona desert. Horses broke down and died, only a little corn could be bought from the occasional Indians, and water holes were far apart. But the trails led to better country and the last days were easier, though rations ran entirely out.

THE SPANISH ARRIVAL AT CÍBOLA

The Indians had them under observation and on July 6, 1540 they met some. The commander of the advance point assured the natives that the invasion was peaceful but that night they attacked the camp, causing confusion but doing no damage. On July 7 the almost starving column, plodding under its dust across the plain, saw a building that no doubt was shining in the sun. It appeared to be made of stone, it was four stories high with setbacks and terraces, and it was large enough to accommodate something less than two hundred families: it was a pueblo. The army had two bushels of corn left and needed a lot more. So Coronado parleyed with the defending chiefs, offering them peace for submission. They were not a warlike people but they didn't care to submit. The army shouted the "Santiago!" with which Spanish troops had launched the charge for

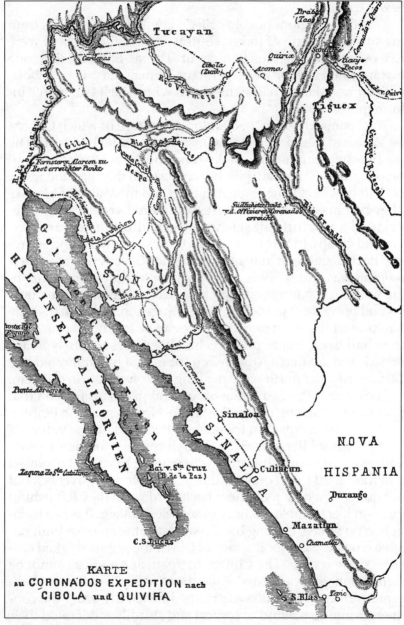

This old map depicts Coronado's expeditions.

centuries and it was soon over. Coronado was twice knocked down by stones from the walls, he got an arrow in his foot, two or three others were wounded, three horses were killed. The chiefs surrendered with quarter and Spain had conquered the Seven Cities.

This was the Zuñi pueblo called Háwikuh, a few miles from the surviving Zuñi of today, southwest of Gallup. There were five other Zuñi pueblos hereabout. The six of them, with one that had vanished or was legendary or imaginary, were Cíbola, which Fray Marcos had named and with which Guzmán's informants had traded.

The Spanish had reached an Indian culture of which Cabeza de Vaca had heard, some of whose products he had seen. The pueblo-dwelling Indians of Arizona and New Mexico were of several tribes. They had a higher civilization than any the Spanish had previously met except in Peru and the Valley of Mexico. They had lived here for at least six hundred years and had developed a magnificent scientific agriculture. Their arts, expressed chiefly in turquoise jewelry, music, pottery, and weaving, have delighted white men ever since Cabeza de Vaca. Their religion was and is noble. A gentle people, they were flourishing when Coronado's soldiers came to count seventy-one pueblos and bring most of them under subjugation, but perhaps they had passed the noon mark. For they were less numerous than they had been, many pueblos had been mysteriously abandoned, and the fierce Athapascan tribes that had migrated like Tartars from the north were pushing their frontiers in on them.

They were dignified, industrious, and peaceful. Too bad that Spain, here reaching one of the farthest frontiers of the Empire, could not attach them in friendship. It could not: the nature of the Spanish soldier and of the Church spiritual forbade. Coronado was . . . an honorable man who wanted a peaceful conquest and tried hard to get one; he almost held his army in check but not quite. When he took them back to Mexico, they left behind them an ineradicable memory of senseless killing. It was a foundation on which, coming back years later, the Spanish built notable cruelties, and for the love of Christ the priests worked cruelties of their own. The Church in Spanish America cannot be summed up in an adjective. After the blood-bath of the first half-century of conquest, heroic priests did steadily bring the conquerors into some kind of control and steadily moderated their inhumanity. The priest was the only defender the Indian had (outside the law courts of Spain itself) against massacre and torture—and yet there were always the doctrines of punishment and obedience, and when heresy or even obstinacy endangered souls which murder might deliver into Heaven, just enforcement of the laws was true mercy. . . . The pueblo dwellers too, like all Indians, had a genius for cruelty and revenge, so for generations the history of New Mexico was stained with blood. But they also had a genius for spiritual and cultural resistance. It has served them well. Today they are still a people, as few other tribes of the United States can be said to be.

A GREAT SHOCK

But to its conquerors Cíbola was a shock so great as almost to unhinge the mind. They saw that these were superior Indians and, thank God, had plenty of corn and beans, but they had expected rooms corded nine feet deep with gold and emeralds. Fray Marcos found it expedient to leave with the first express for Mexico and Coronado wrote to Mendoza that "he has not told the truth in a single thing he said." This was a Spanish New World army: it had expected to be rich by the end of its first charge. To keep it from wreaking its anger on the Indians, which was the way of conquerors, required the finest leadership but Coronado kept his men in hand.

He set about exploring the land and hunting for the treasure that must be somewhere. One reconnaissance reached the kingdom of Tontonteac north of Zuñi, about which Estéban [a Moor who accompanied Fray Marcos on the first Cíbola expedition] had heard. Its seven rich cities turned out to be a cluster of Hopi pueblos, again with full granaries but no treasure. Another one set out for a great river which the Hopis had described and, under García López de Cárdenas, a violent man but a brilliant commander, reached the rim of the Grand Canyon. A third marched eastward to another kingdom, called Tiguex, which turned out to be the center of the pueblo culture, the valley of the Rio Grande upstream from Cabeza de Vaca's passage. Thence, it pushed on to the eastern outpost of the culture, the pueblo of Pecos, where it got news of the buffalo herds and made a momentous captive, an Indian who was a prisoner of the pueblo and whom the Spanish called "the Turk." A fourth, commanded by Melchior Díaz, went west to the Colorado River, where it found messages from the ships commanded by Alarcón. . . .

FAILURE AND SUCCESS

Considering that the Spanish had had only one purpose in 1540, the expedition was indeed an absolute failure. It so shattered one particular dream of gold that the still luminous myth of Quivira had to flee a thousand miles northwest to the shore of the Pacific, and no one started toward Cíbola [a pueblo that the Spanish called "New Peru" because it was reputed—falsely— to contain many riches] again for forty years. . . .

But only in that Coronado found no treasure did his expedition fail. Few explorations in all American history were better led, few dealt more successfully with the problems of wilderness travel. And no one had preceded it, it was the first that passed this way, it could call on no distillation of other men's experiences, every emergency it met was strange and every place it traveled to was new. Thus early the exploration of interior North America sounds a high clear note. Coronado was so aware of what he was doing and so competent at meeting the challenge of the wilderness that, although mirage and myth had led him here, he seems a critical intelligence supported by exact knowledge.

CORONADO'S ARRIVAL AT CÍBOLA

PEDRO CASTAÑEDA

Pedro Castañeda, a soldier of the Coronado expedition to what is now the southwestern United States, recalls the expedition's disappointing discovery of the famed city of Cíbola, one of the Seven Cities reputed by the Spanish to contain many riches. In reality, Cíbola was a crowded Indian pueblo containing nothing of value to the Spaniards other than food. According to Castañeda, in spite of the pueblos' lack of gold, Coronado and his men fought the Indians for control of the village.

G eneral Francisco de Coronado, as has been said, started to continue his journey from the valley of Culiacan somewhat lightly equipped, taking with him the friars, since none of them wished to stay behind with the army. After they had gone three days, a regular friar who could say mass, named Friar Antonio Victoria, broke his leg, and they brought him back from the camp to have it doctored. He stayed with the army after this, which was no slight consolation for all. The general and his force crossed the country without trouble, as they found everything peaceful, because the Indians knew Friar Marcos and some of the others who had been with Melchior Diaz when he went with Juan de Saldibar to investigate [the region before Coronado's expedition].

DISAPPOINTMENTS

After the general had crossed the inhabited region and came to Chichilticalli, where the wilderness begins, and saw nothing fa-

Pedro Castañeda, *The Journey of Coronado*, Ann Arbor, MI: University Microfilms, Inc., 1966.

vorable, he could not help feeling somewhat downhearted, for, although the reports were very fine about what was ahead, there was nobody who had seen it except the Indians who went with the negro [named Esteban who had gone with Fray Marcos], and these had already been caught in some lies. Besides all this, he was much affected by seeing that the fame of Chichilticalli was summed up in one tumble-down house without any roof, although it appeared to have been a strong place at some former time when it was inhabited, and it was very plain that it had been built by a civilized and warlike race of strangers who had come from a distance. This building was made of red earth. From here they went on through the wilderness, and in fifteen days came to a river about 8 leagues from Cibola, which they called Red River, because its waters were muddy and reddish. In this river they found mullets like those of Spain. The first Indians from that country were seen here—two of them, who ran away to give the news. During the night following the next day, about 2 leagues from the village, some Indians in a safe place yelled so that, although the men were ready for anything, some were so excited that they put their saddles on hindside before; but these were the new fellows. When the veterans had mounted and ridden round the camp, the Indians fled. None of them could be caught because they knew the country.

The next day they entered the settled country in good order, and when they saw the first village, which was Cibola, such were the curses that some hurled at Friar Marcos that I pray God may protect him from them.

It is a little, crowded village, looking as if it had been crumpled all up together. There are ranch houses in New Spain which make a better appearance at a distance. It is a village of about 200 warriors, is three and four stories high, with the houses small and having only a few rooms, and without a courtyard. One yard serves for each section. The people of the whole district had collected here, for there are seven villages in the province, and some of the others are even larger and stronger than Cibola. These folks waited for the army, drawn up by divisions in front of the village. When they refused to have peace on the terms the interpreters extended to them, but appeared defiant, the Santiago [a war cry addressed to Saint James] was given, and they were at once put to flight. The Spaniards then attacked the village, which was taken with not a little difficulty, since they held the narrow and crooked entrance. During the attack they knocked the general down with a large stone, and would have killed him but for Don Garcia Lopez de Cardenas and Hernando de Alvarado, who threw themselves above him and drew him away, receiving the blows of the stones, which were not few. But the first fury of the Spaniards could not be resisted, and in less than an hour they entered the village and captured it. They discovered food there, which was the thing they were most in need of. After this the whole province was at peace.

CORONADO TELLS THE KING OF HIS FAILED EXPEDITION

Francisco Vásquez de Coronado

In 1540, Francisco Vásquez de Coronado led an expedition to what is now the southwestern United States in search of rich empires to conquer for Spain. On October 20, 1541, about a year and a half after beginning the journey, Coronado wrote a letter to king of Spain Charles V relating the reason he was aborting the expedition. According to Coronado, the Spaniards had discovered only poor Indians and their crude villages, and they had no reason to believe that further exploration would be fruitful.

H oly Catholic Cæsarian Majesty: On April 20, [1541] of this year, I wrote to Your Majesty from this province of Tiguex, in reply to a letter from Your Majesty dated in Madrid, June 11, [1540] a year ago. I gave a detailed account of this expedition, which the viceroy of New Spain ordered me to undertake in Your Majesty's name to this country which was discovered by Fray Marcos de Niza, the provincial of the order of Saint Francis. I described it all, and the sort of force I have, as Your Majesty had ordered me to relate in my letters; and stated that while I was engaged in the conquest and pacification of the natives of this province, some Indians who were natives of other provinces beyond these had told me that in their country there were much larger villages and better houses than those of the natives of this country, and that they had lords who ruled

Francisco Vásquez de Coronado, "Letter from Francisco Vasquez de Coronado to His Majesty, Charles V, October 20, 1541," *North American Discovery: Circa 1000–1612*, Columbia: University of South Carolina Press, 1971.

them, who were served with dishes of gold, and other very magnificent things; and although, as I wrote to Your Majesty, I did not believe it before I had set eyes on it, because it was the report of Indians and given for the most part by means of signs, yet as the report appeared to me to be very valuable and that it was important that it should be investigated for Your Majesty's service, I determined to go and see it with the men I have here. I started from this province [of Tiguex] on the 23rd of last April [1540], for the place where the Indians wanted to guide me. After nine days' march I reached some plains, so vast that I did not find their limit anywhere that I went, although I marched over them for more than 300 leagues. And I found such a quantity of cows [buffalo] in these, of the kind that I wrote Your Majesty about, which they have in this country, that it is impossible to number them, for while I was journeying through these plains, until I returned to where I first found them, there was not a day that I lost sight of them.

THE QUERECHOS AND THE TEYAS

And after seventeen days' march I came to a settlement of Indians who are called Querechos, who travel around with these cows, who do not plant, and who eat the raw flesh and drink the blood of the cows they kill, and they tan the skins of the cows, with which all the people of this country dress themselves here. They have little field tents made of the hides of the cows, tanned and greased, very well made, in which they live while they travel around near the cows, moving with these. They have dogs which they load, which carry their tents and poles and belongings. These people have the best figures of any that I have seen in the Indies [the name the Spanish gave to the New World]. They could not give me any account of the country where the guides were taking me. I traveled five days more as the guides wished to lead me, until I reached some plains, with no more landmarks than as if we had been swallowed up in the sea, where they strayed about, because there was not a stone, nor a bit of rising ground, nor a tree, nor a shrub, nor anything to go by. There is much very fine pasture land, with good grass. And while we were lost in these plains, some horsemen who went off to hunt cows fell in with some Indians who also were out hunting, who are enemies of those that I had seen in the last settlement, and of another sort of people who are called Teyas; they have their bodies and faces all painted, are a large people like the others, of a very good build; they eat the raw flesh just like the Querechos, and live and travel round with the cows in the same way as these. I obtained from these an account of the country where the guides were taking me, which was not like what they had told me, because these made out that the houses there were not built of stones, with stories, as my guides had described it, but of straw and skins, and a small supply of corn there.

This news troubled me greatly, to find myself on these limitless plains, where I was in great need of water, and often had to drink it so poor that it was more mud than water. Here the guides confessed to me that they had not told the truth in regard to the size of the houses, because these were of straw, but that they had done so regarding the large number of inhabitants and the other things about their habits. The Teyas disagreed with this, and on account of this division between some of the Indians and the others, and also because many of the men I had with me had not eaten anything except meat for some days, because we had reached the end of the corn which we carried from this province [of Tiguex], and because they made it out more than forty days' journey from where I fell in with the Teyas to the country where the guides were taking me, although I appreciated the trouble and danger there would be in the journey owing to the lack of water and corn, it seemed to me best, in order to see if there was anything there of service to Your Majesty, to go forward with only 30 horsemen until I should be able to see the country, so as to give Your Majesty a true account of what was to be found in it. I sent all the rest of the force I had with me to this province, with Don Tristán de Arellano in command, because it would have been impossible to prevent the loss of many men, if all had gone on, owing to the lack of water and because they also had to kill bulls and cows on which to sustain themselves.

And with only the 30 horsemen whom I took for my escort, I traveled forty-two days after I left the force, living all this while solely on the flesh of the bulls and cows which we killed, at the cost of several of our horses which they killed, because, as I wrote Your Majesty, they are very brave and fierce animals; and going many days without water, and cooking the food with cow dung, because there is not any kind of wood in all these plains, away from the gullies and rivers, which are very few.

It was the Lord's pleasure that, after having journeyed across these deserts seventy-seven days, I arrived at the province they call Quivira, to which the guides were conducting me, and where they had described to me houses of stone, with many stories; and not only are they not of stone, but of straw, but the people in them are as barbarous as all those whom I have seen and passed before this; they do not have cloaks, nor cotton of which to make these, but use the skins of the cattle they kill, which they tan, because they are settled among these on a very large river. They eat the raw flesh like the Querechos and Teyas; they are enemies of one another, but are all of the same sort of people, and these at Quivira have the advantage in the houses they build and in planting corn. In this province of which the guides who brought me are natives, they received me peaceably, and although they told me when I set out for it that I could not succeed in seeing it all in two months, there are not more than 25 villages of straw houses there and in all the rest of the country that I saw and learned about, which gave their obedience to Your Majesty and placed themselves under your royal overlordship. The people here are large. I had several Indians measured, and found that they were 10 palms [80 inches] in height; the women are well proportioned and their features are more like Moorish women than Indians. The natives here gave me a piece of copper which a chief Indian wore hung around his neck; I sent it to the viceroy of New Spain [Mexico], because I have not seen any other metal in these parts except this and some little copper bells which I sent him, and a bit of metal which looks like gold. I do not know where this came from, although I believe that the Indians who gave it to me obtained it from those whom I brought here in my service, because I can not find any other origin for it nor where it came from.

The diversity of languages which exists in this country and my not having anyone who understood them, because they speak their own language in each village, has hindered me, because I have been forced to send captains and men in many directions to find out whether there was anything in this country which could be of service to Your Majesty. And although I have searched with all diligence I have not found or heard of anything, unless it be these provinces, which are a very small affair. The province of Quivira is 950 leagues from Mexico. Where I reached it, it is in the fortieth degree. The country itself is the best I have ever seen for producing all the products of Spain, for besides the land itself being very fat and black and being very well watered by the rivulets and springs and rivers, I found plums like those of Spain and nuts and very good sweet grapes and mulberries. I have treated the natives of this province, and all the others whom I found wherever I went, as well as was possible, agreeably to what Your Majesty had commanded, and they have received no harm in any way from me or from those who went in my company. I remained twenty-five days in this province of Quivira, so as to see and explore the country and also to find out whether there was anything beyond which could be of service to Your Majesty, because the guides who had brought me had given me an account of other provinces beyond this. And what I am sure of is that there is not any gold nor any other metal in all that country, and the other things of which they had told me are nothing but little villages, and in many of these they do not plant anything and do not have any houses except of skins and sticks, and they wander around with the cows; so that the account they gave me was false, because they wanted to persuade me to go there with the whole force, believing that as the way was through such uninhabited deserts, and from the lack of water, they would get us where we and our horses would die of hunger. And the guides confessed this, and said they had done it by the advice and orders of the natives of these provinces.

FAILURE AND DISAPPOINTMENT

At this, after having heard the account of what was beyond, which I have given above, I returned to these provinces to provide for the force I had sent back here and to give Your Majesty an account of what this country amounts to, because I wrote Your Majesty that I would do so when I went there. I have done all that I possibly could to serve Your Majesty and to discover a country where God Our Lord might be served and the royal patrimony of Your Majesty increased, as your loyal servant and vassal. For since I reached the province of Cíbola, to which the viceroy of New Spain sent me in the name of Your Majesty, seeing that there were none of the things there of which Friar Marcos had told, I have managed to explore this country for 200 leagues and more around Cíbola, and the best place I have found is this river of Tiguex where I am now, and the settlements here. It would not be possible to establish a settlement here, for besides being 400 leagues from the North sea and more than 200 from the South sea, with which it is impossible to have any sort of communication, the country is so cold, as I have written to Your Majesty, that apparently the winter could not possibly be spent here, because there is no wood, nor cloth with which to protect the men, except the skins which the natives wear and some small amount of cotton cloaks. I send the viceroy of New Spain an account of everything I have seen in the countries where I have been, and as Don García López de Cárdenas is going to kiss Your Majesty's hands, who has done much and has served Your Majesty very well on this expedition, and he will give Your Majesty an account of everything here, as one who has seen it himself, I give way to him. And may Our Lord protect the Holy Imperial Catholic person of Your Majesty, with increase of greater kingdoms and powers, as your loyal servants and vassals desire. From this province of Tiguex, October 20, in the year 1541.

FRANCISCO VÁZQUEZ DE CORONADO

THE PUEBLO

A. GROVE DAY

A. Grove Day, who was a history professor at the University of California, Berkeley, wrote many books, including *Coronado's Quest: The Discovery of the Southwestern States*, from which the following excerpt was taken. Day describes the Hopi and Zuni Indians—whom the Spanish named Pueblo Indians—at the time when Spanish explorer Francisco Vásquez de Coronado began exploring Arizona and New Mexico in 1540. The Pueblos were unlike other Indians in North America in that they had given up the nomadic life and settled into established villages and grew corn to support themselves. Pueblo societies were communal, and, to the surprise of the Spaniards, they had no kings or aristocrats. The Hopi and Zuni Indians built their pueblos in out-of-the-way places that could be easily defended, and the honeycomb design of their earthen dwellings further protected them. According to Day, because the Pueblo Indians were sedentary, they were able to perfect such arts as pottery making and weaving.

T he Zuñi settlements, where [Spanish explorer Francisco de] Coronado was to spend some months [in 1540] directing the exploration of the surrounding territories, were the first towns of the sedentary tribes of the Southwest in which the members of the expedition lived, and of which they gave descriptions. Among all the achievements of the Coronado expedition, not the least is that he and his men first gave to the world an account of these Pueblo Indians, who still retain the name given them by the Spaniards.

The Pueblo Indians, like their ancestors, the cliff dwellers [Anasazi], sprang from the same basic stock as the other Amer-

A. Grove Day, *Coronado's Quest: The Discovery of the Southwestern States*, Berkeley: University of California Press, 1940. Copyright © 1940 by the Regents of the University of California. Reproduced by permission.

ican races. They did differ sharply from all other tribes of the continent north of Mexico in that they had forsaken the nomad life of hunters following herds of game over vast territories, and had chosen rather to settle in easily defended valleys and to depend on the soil for their living. The agricultural life that they led gave rise to differences still more marked; they built permanent houses, created a village society, were able to store up food and other forms of wealth, and had leisure to create works of art and to develop an intricate ritual of worship.

By 1540, when Coronado first met these descendants of the cliff dwellers, the Pueblo Indians had developed a native American democratic culture of such deep-rooted strength that in spite of later vicissitudes it was never lost to them. The Coronado chronicles give an excellent picture of this culture. The Spanish records reveal a high respect for the Indian achievements, which is the more remarkable considering the fact that the invaders could have had only the vaguest notion of the true attainments of the Indians and their tribal aspirations.

COMMUNITIES, NOT KINGDOMS

It is one of the strongest traits of the Indian to be secretive regarding his feelings, or any of his activities which reflect religious or social ideals. Moreover, the Indian culture is almost Oriental in its mystical acceptance of religion and art as the predominating factors of life, in its traditional submergence of individual desire into communal welfare, and in its tranquil idealization of spiritual attainments and disdain of mere material advantage. Hence it was well-nigh impossible for a conquering European, coming from a crowded land of kings and priests and merchants warring for gains that could be made only at the expense of another's loss, to comprehend—or even to be aware of—the main currents in a way of life so markedly strange to him. What was one to do with a people without a "king," who had no rulers or aristocrats or conquerors or rich men or self-seeking individualists, whose meanest utensil was a work of art, who did not fear death and yet whose smallest act was always an act of worship?

Each of the pueblos was an independent republic. "They do not have chiefs as in New Spain, but are ruled by a council of the oldest men," wrote [Pedro] Castañeda [who was a soldier in Coronado's expedition]. "They have priests who preach to them, whom they call *papas*. These are the elders. They go up on the highest roof of the village and preach to the village from there, like public criers, in the morning while the sun is rising, the whole village being silent and sitting in the galleries to listen. They tell them how they are to live, and I believe that they give certain commandments for them to keep, for there is no drunkenness among them nor sodomy nor sacrifices, neither do they eat human flesh nor steal, but they are usually at work." There was little crime in the modern meaning of the word. Land, so often in other civilizations a cause of quarrels, was not held by individuals; all the lands were owned by the village, and allotted in accordance with family needs. In times of scarcity, the hardships were shared by everyone in the community alike, and none starved until all starved.

Although the village was divided into totemic clans (or clusters of families related through a common maternal ancestor), the community was the social unit. So far as is known, there has never been in the history of the Pueblo people any political group larger than a temporary alliance of tribes, which fell apart as soon as the common danger was past. The village was self-contained, and there was little trade with other provinces except in such things as the sacred turquoise. Another barrier to the mingling of tribes was the fact that within a small territory two villages might speak languages as different as French is from German, although, when necessary, the highly descriptive sign language that later amazed Coronado served as a lingua franca among the tribes.

REVERENCE FOR NATURE

Like all Indians, those of the pueblos worshiped the elements—in particular the creative sun, whose priests were to be seen praying at dawn. Sun and water and cloud manifestly dominated the destinies of these tillers of the arid lands. Even on the darker side, their religion was a fetishism based on fear of the elements; the medicine man and the greatly feared "witch" were looked upon as having power over natural events.

All their arts—and every pueblo dweller was an artist—were reflections of their spirit of gratitude and reverence for these life-giving forces. The great communal art was that of the dance—sun dances, rain dances, growing-corn dances—dramas accompanied by the music of pipes and drums, performed in ceremonial garments and symbolic masks, and prefaced by the making of priest-drawn "sand paintings" of vivid pigments and ground meal. The designs of their famous basketry and pottery were always symbolic, as were those of the laboriously woven, bright blankets of cotton. The lovely symmetry of the pottery was achieved by skilled handcraft, for the potter's wheel was unknown to them and even today is never used. Each stage of any of their work was done with deliberate perfection, for time meant almost nothing to these leisurely people who, unlike their southern brothers in Mexico, had never developed a calendar.

Even the hunting of beasts—deer, bear, mountain lion, buffalo, wild turkey, the humble rabbit—must be undertaken with proper ceremony. Fish, as sacred to the water gods, were never eaten.

Water was the great determiner of their lives, for in the bleached and dusty plateau land every drop is precious, and settlements are only possible along the trickling streams. The greatest dances, such as the Snake Dance of the Hopis of Tusayán, were those imploring the life-giving rains. When these came, the intensive cultivation of corn, pumpkins, and beans could enable the growers to store up enough to feed themselves for another year or two. Irrigation was practiced on a small scale, but any prolonged drought meant catastrophe. Every expedient to catch and store the precious fluid was used, and each village had a *tinaja*, or cistern, wherever there was a proper depression in the rock.

Maize, their only cereal, was the staff of life among the Pueblos, and a good crop might last them for several years, for in the dry air the kernels did not rot. The corn at Zuñi in particular impressed the Spaniards greatly; many of the army had been farmers themselves and knew good plants when they saw them. "It does not grow very high," remarked Castañeda. "The ears start at the very foot, and each large fat stalk bears about eight hundred grains, something not seen before in our parts." Coronado found it an appetizing staple of diet. "They make the best corn cakes I have ever seen anywhere," he wrote, "and this is what everybody ordinarily eats. They have the very best arrangement and equipment for grinding that was ever seen. One of these Indian women here will grind as much as four of the Mexicans."

A PEACEFUL PEOPLE

The Pueblo Indians were able fighters, although they did not expect to make a trade of fighting for gain, as did their wandering, raiding enemies the Apaches. There were also occasional battles between two or more of their villages, and the war chiefs were at such times the leaders in council. During aggressive raids—when the warriors often wore round-soled war sandals whose tracks would give no indication of the direction taken by the wearer—the young men obtained training in the arts of fighting, and at home had always to be continually on the alert against marauding bands. The Pueblos, like other Indians, took scalps; at Zuñi, the dried hanging scalps of victims were used as a gruesome sort of barometer, for the skin became soft and pliable at the approach of rain. However, by temperament the pueblo dwellers preferred to live in seclusion and peace, and they fought best on the defensive.

The home places of these town builders were always chosen for defensive reasons. Most of the villages were found in localities that were grim, almost barren, frequently sandy and hot, and at long distances from their hunting grounds. Many lovely forest glades of the Southwest show no trace of permanent Indian occupation; Coronado passed through the wooded country of the White Mountains, but found there only a few prowling savages. The reason for this was that in order to stay for any length of time in a region the southwestern Indian required not only availability of water, cultivable soil, and timber, but most of all security. The high forests of New Mexico and Arizona, aside from being hard to grub out for planting, as well as being exceedingly cold and snowbound in winter, provided excellent lurking places for nomad raiders. The village Indian was willing to carry his wood and water from a distance, and even to travel to fertile patches of land and camp there through the growing season, so long as he could find protection when it was needed. For his permanent home, therefore, he built strong-walled houses that could withstand a siege.

It was not until the Spaniards came that the full strength of these fortress towns was fully tested, for most of the attacks of other Indians were of short duration. Protection was offered by some villages because they were built in out-of-the-way spots secluded from enemy observation. In some places, the walls of the houses blended into the rocky landscape and were not noticeable. Other towns were built on crags or mesas that were hard for an enemy to scale. Watchtowers were often erected on the borders of a tribal range so that watchers could give ample warning of the approach of a raiding party. Often a tribe unwilling to do battle would be able to abandon its houses and scatter to secret places of refuge for a few days, until danger was past.

The fortress towns of the Pueblos were always built in strategic spots, even though this might mean that most of their food and water, and even garden soil, had to be carried in jars and baskets up almost perpendicular trails worn deep in stone by generations of moccasined feet. Much of their building material, especially the large framing timbers, had to be transported for great distances. Where building stone was plentiful, the Indians built in stone, selected for smooth shattered faces but not dressed with tools; otherwise they used puddled masses of sundried clay, joined with a native mortar and white-washed with chalky gypsum.

PUEBLO ARCHITECTURE

A village grew as adjoining rooms from time to time were added like the cells in a honeycomb. Outer walls had neither doors nor windows; easily withdrawn ladders, which were removed to baffle attackers, led from terrace to terrace; the rooms of the various families were entered by openings in the ceilings, "like hatchways of ships."

The heart of the village was always the *kiva*—the Hopi Indian name for the chamber that the first Spaniards called *estufa* (literally "stove," but meaning also "hot-room" or "hot-bath"). These pine-pillared underground rooms were built only by the men and were always barred to women. Often rather spacious, the dark sanctums served as church, clubroom, school for boys, and lodge hall for male secret societies. Other small shrines were built in secret places out of doors.

The dress of these Indians was as distinctive as their dwellings. The typical garb of the male members of the Pueblo tribes was a short tunic, trousers, leggings, and moccasins, all of tanned deerskin, with a decorated skin cap. Robes of woven yucca fiber, rabbit skin, or mountain-lion skin were worn in cold weather, as well as feather cloaks or bright cotton blankets, woven by both men and women and worn on gala days. The men cut their hair in bangs in front, and plaited it on the side or held it back with a headband. The women wore a blanket-like woven garment thrown over the right shoulder and under the left, and belted with a wide sash; a woven shirt; and leggings and moccasins like those of the men. Their hair was usually parted in the middle and hung in braids; girls who had reached the marriageable age wore disk-shaped puffs on each side of the head. Both sexes decorated their persons with sacred turquoise and drilled-shell ornaments hung from ear and neck, or attached to belts and leggings. Earth pigments served for painting the body for the many dances and other tribal ceremonies.

To such a self-sufficient people, the invading Spaniards had little to offer in the way of "civilizing" implements or influences. True, they implanted in the country a diversity of domestic animals (the Indians had only the dog and the turkey), particularly the horse and the sheep. But the exchange between red man and white has never been one-sided. If anything, the Pueblo Indian has given more than he has received. His lore and craftsmanship and painfully won wisdom of existence have passed into the American heritage. His way of building a home, for example, created a style that is still furnishing inspiration to architecture in the western states. The Indian culture, like his dwellings, has remained firmly rooted in the soil that Coronado's army trod. Today, any visitor to the American Southwest may see this enduring race living virtually as they lived when Coronado came, four centuries ago.

THE FOUR FLUTES: A ZUNI MYTH

TRADITIONAL

When Coronado came into contact with the Zuni in 1540, he found them to be a peaceful, artistic people. One of the arts they were noted for was dance. Because the Zuni grew maize in the arid region which is now New Mexico, many of their ceremonial dances involved tributes to the god of water. According to the following legend, the Zuni people wished for new music and dances, so they sent four Wise Ones to visit the God of Dew to ask about his music-making secrets. Paíyatuma performed beautiful music for the Wise Ones and gave each one a flute. With these flutes, the Zuni people were able to make new music and create new dances.

H ow the Zuñis wished for new music and new dances for their people when they participated in ceremonials! But they knew not how to create their wishes into realities.

Their Chief and his counselors decided to ask their Old Grandfathers for help. They journeyed to the Elder Priests of the Bow and asked, "Grandfathers, we are tired of the same old music and the old dances. Can you please show us how to make new music and new dances for our people?"

After much conferring, the Elder Priests arranged to send our Wise Ones to visit the God of Dew. Next day the four Wise Ones set out upon their mission.

THE WISE ONES VISIT RAINBOW CAVE

Slowly climbing a steep trail, they were pleased to hear music coming from the high Sacred Mountain. Near the top, they dis-

Traditional, "The Four Flutes," *Voices of the Winds: Native American Legends*, New York: Facts On File, 1989.

covered that the music came from the Cave of the Rainbow. At the cave's entrance, vapors floated about, a sign that within was the god Paíyatuma.

When the four Wise Ones asked permission to go in, the music stopped; however, they were welcomed warmly by Paíyatuma, who said, "Our musicians will now rest while we learn why you have come."

"Our Elders, the Priests of the Bow, directed us to you. We wish for you to show us your secret in making new sounds of music. Also with the new music, we wish to learn how to create new ceremonial dances.

"As gifts, our Elders have prepared these prayer sticks and special plume-offerings for you and your people."

"Come sit with me," responded Paíyatuma. "You shall now see and hear."

Before them appeared many musicians with beautifully decorated long shirts. Their faces were painted with the signs of the gods. Each held a lengthy tapered flute. In the center of the group was a large drum, beside which stood its drum-beater. Another musician held the conductor's wand. These were men of age and experience, graced with dignity.

Paíyatuma stood and spread some magic pollen at the feet of the visiting Wise Ones. With crossed arms, he then strode the length of the cave, turning and walking back again. Seven beautiful young girls, tall and slender, followed him. Their garments were similar to the musicians, but were of various colors. They held hollow cottonwood shafts from which bubbled dainty clouds when the maidens blew into them.

"These are not the maidens of corn," Paíyatuma said. "They are our dancers, the young sisters from the House of Stars."

Paíyatuma placed a flute to his lips and joined the circle of dancers. From the drum came a thunderous beat, shaking the entire Cave of the Rainbow, signaling the performance to begin.

BEAUTIFUL MUSIC

Beautiful music from the flutes seemed to sing and sigh like the gentle blowing of the winds. Bubbles of vapor arose from the girls' reeds. In rhythm, the Butterflies of Summerland flew about the cave, creating their own dance forms with the dancers and the musicians. Mysteriously, over all the scene flooded the colors of the Rainbow throughout the cave. All of this harmony seemed like a dream to the four Wise Ones, as they thanked the

God of Dew and prepared to leave.

Paíyatuma came forward with a benevolent smile and symbolically breathed upon the four Wise Ones. He summoned four musicians, asking them to give each one a flute as a gift.

"Now depart to your Elders," said Paíyatuma. "Tell them what you have seen and heard. Give them our flutes. May your people the Zuñis learn to sing like the birds through these woodwinds and these reeds."

In gratitude the Wise Ones bowed deeply and accepted the gifts, expressing their appreciation and farewell to all of the performers and Paíyatuma.

Upon the return of the four Wise Ones to their own ceremonial court, they placed the four flutes before the Priests of the Bow. The Wise Ones described and demonstrated all that they had seen and heard in the Cave of the Rainbow.

Chief of the Zuñi tribe and his counselors were happy with their new knowledge, returning to their tribe with the gift of the flutes and the reeds. Before their next ceremonial, many of their tribesmen learned to make new music and to create new dances for all their people to enjoy.

CABRILLO EXPLORES THE CALIFORNIA COAST

ROBERT KIRSCH AND WILLIAM S. MURPHY

In the following selection, Robert Kirsch and William S. Murphy relate details of Juan Rodríguez Cabrillo's expedition up the coast of California in 1542. According to the authors, Cabrillo was the first European to see California, which many Spaniards believed was a land of riches and a possible passage from North America to the Orient. Unfortunately for Cabrillo, he discovered neither riches nor a passage to China, and his contemporaries considered his expedition a failure. However, Kirsch and Murphy note that Cabrillo has since been credited with maintaining peaceful relations with the Indians he met during his explorations of San Diego Bay, Santa Monica Bay, and the Channel Islands. Cabrillo died mid-voyage on the Channel Island of San Miguel. Robert Kirsch is a novelist and William S. Murphy is the author of several books on California, including *West of the West: Witness to the California Experience, 1542–1906*, a project he coauthored with Kirsch. The following excerpt was taken from *West of the West*.

W hat is now California was discovered in one of the minor thrusts of [the Spanish surge of exploration and conquest during the sixteenth century]. The first Europeans known to have set foot on this land, and whom we can identify, were under the command of Juan Rodríguez Cabrillo, a seasoned professional, one of that band of original conquistadores who served Hernando Cortés in the campaign that conquered Aztec Mexico between 1519 and 1521. Probably a native of Portugal, Cabrillo's fame as the discoverer of Alta California came long after his death. By that time much of the specific detail about him had been lost. California was considered marginal; its wealth was not obvious to the land-sated Spanish. Later it would become a way station for the treasure ships sailing from the Philippines to Mexico. That alone ensured the land and its Indian inhabitants a relatively undisturbed period of more than two hundred years.

THE DISCOVERY OF SAN DIEGO

By 1542, when Cabrillo sailed with his two crude ships from the Port of Natividad on the west coast of Mexico, the great spasm of exploration and conquest had lost its major thrust. Obscure men were being sent to test out the dreams of El Dorado [an imaginary region in the Americas supposedly unsurpassed in riches, especially gold] and the theories of a Northwest Passage, which the Spaniards called the Strait of Anian [thought to be a route to the Orient]. The peninsula of Baja California was then, and for decades thereafter, believed to be an island off the fabled Indies.

Against prevailing northwesterlies, Cabrillo's two ships took three months to beat up to what is now San Diego Bay. The first recorded sight of California comes from the report of that voyage. The document bears the name of Bartolomeo Ferrelo, Cabrillo's pilot, a Levantine [Syrian] sailor who succeeded to the command of the ships after the death of Cabrillo. It was written in the third person, and describes the events of September 27 and 28, 1542:

> On this day they saw on the mainland some great smokes. The country appears to be good, with large valleys. Inside, there are some high sierras.
>
> On Thursday they sailed about six leagues along a north-north-west coast and discovered a very good closed port in 34°20', which they named San Miguel. After anchoring they went ashore where there were some people three of whom awaited them, while the rest fled. To these some presents were given, and they explained by signs that inland people like the Spaniards had passed, and they displayed much fear. That night some went ashore from the ships to fish with a net, and it seems that there were some Indians who commenced

to shoot arrows at them and wounded three men. The following day in the morning they went with the ship's boat farther up into the port, which is large, and brought back two boys who understood nothing by signs; they gave them some shirts and shortly sent them away. The following day in the morning three large Indians came to the ships and explained by signs that some people like us, that is bearded, dressed and armed like those aboard the vessels, were going about inland. They showed by signs that these carried cross-bows, and swords; they made gestures with the right arm as if using lances, and went running about as if they were going on horseback, and further showed that these were killing many of the native Indians, and for this reason they were afraid. The people were well-built and large and go about covered with the skins of animals. While in this port a great tempest passed over, but nothing of it was felt as the port is so good. It was from the west-southwest and the southwest and violent. They were in this port until the following Tuesday; here they call the Christians *Guacamal.*

On Tuesday following, October 3, they left San Miguel . . .

San Miguel did not take hold as a place name. Years afterward it would be known by its later christening, San Diego. The tone of the report and its lack of excitement indicate something about Cabrillo and the nature of his voyage. There was nothing about the captain that suggested the ambition or prominence of his late commander, Hernando Cortés, or the hero Pedro de Alvarado, who was to have commanded the 1542 expedition originally. Cabrillo was reliable, responsible, and judging from the sentiments expressed by his crew after his death, a good captain. . . .

A MAN OF PEACE

We do not know the specific instructions [given to Cabrillo by Viceroy Antonio de Mendoza], although it seems likely that the same general purposes that were given for earlier expeditions remained in force: Find the Strait of Anian, locate good harbors, Christianize the Indians, and, as always, stated or unstated, find treasure.

They left Natividad on June 27, 1542. It was the worst season for such a voyage and it took the two ships three months to reach what is now San Diego. The ships were primitive, the crews poorly trained, and there were no charts or maps. Yet Cabrillo seems to have kept the morale of his men high; certainly they respected his ability and courage.

Something of the man emerges in the pages of Ferrelo's journals. Three men were wounded by Indians at the "very good closed port of San Miguel," yet Cabrillo did not order his crews to return fire. This bespeaks good discipline. More than that, he seems to understand the cause of the "much fear" of the Indians, stemming from the "people like the Spaniards" who had been seen inland. . . . Cabrillo had evidently seen enough of bloodshed and violence. His treatment of the Indians is in sharp contrast to that of many of his contemporaries, though not, if Cortés' policies are carefully scrutinized, completely at odds with others'. It should be remembered that Cortés' conquest of Mexico was made possible because of his diplomatic treatment of the enemies of the Aztecs who, in turn, offered substantial assistance in the campaign of the Conquest.

In any case, Cabrillo's peaceful methods worked. They sailed from San Miguel on October 3, landed on one of the Channel Islands (probably Catalina) on the 7th. Ferrelo reports (remember that the journal is written in the third person):

> As the boat was nearing land a great number of Indians came out of the bushes and grass, shouting, dancing, making signs to come ashore. As from the boats they saw the women fleeing, they made signs to them not to fear; so shortly they became assured and put their bows and arrows on the ground. Launching into the water a fine canoe containing eight or ten Indians, they came out to the ships. These were given some beads and presents with which they were well pleased. . . . The Spaniards afterwards went ashore and both the Indian men and women and everybody felt very secure.

On the 8th of October, "they came to the mainland in a large bay, which they named Baia de los Fumos on account of the many smokes they saw there." This has been said to be the Bay of present-day Santa Monica, although there is a possibility that it was present-day San Pedro. They followed the coast, describing it with substantial accuracy. On October 10, they anchored off present-day Ventura, "saw on land an Indian town close to the sea with large houses like that of New Spain [Mexico]." Again the Indians reported the presence of Spaniards inland. Cabrillo sent two men inland. They saw a large town that they called Pueblo de las Canoas, and a "very beautiful valley" where there "was much maize and food."

At least twenty-five Indian towns are given by name. "They are in a good country with fine plains and many trees." The Indians are friendly in this "well-settled" area. "They go dressed in skins and have very long hair tied up with some long cords. Inserted between the hair and these cords are many daggers made of flint, bone and wood."

THE FATEFUL INJURY

Unfavorable winds just past Point Concepción forced them out to sea and they took refuge in a port on the Channel Island of San Miguel. They called it La Posesión. It was here Cabrillo broke his arm. The injury would lead to his death, on this very island some months later. They left the island on October 25, and the sailing difficulties continued. One day there was no wind, the next, an onshore wind drove them toward the coast. It was depressing. " During this month they found the weather on this coast from 34° up, like that in Spain, very cold in the mornings and afternoons and with great storms of rain, heavy clouds, great darkness and heavy air."

If they praised the land, wrote favorably of the Indians, disappointment creeps through. Is there an ironic echo of the Amazon queen of an island of treasure [legend had it that California was a rich land ruled by Amazons] in the following?

> This town at the Puerto de las Sardinas is called *Cicacut*, and the others from there to the Cabo de Galera are: Ciacut, Anacot, Maquinanoa, Palatre, Anocoac, Olesino, Caacac, Paltocac, Tocane, Opia, Opistopia, Nocos, Yutum, Quiman, Micoma, and Garomisopona. The chief of these towns is an old Indian woman who came on board the ships and slept two nights in the *capitana*. . . .

There are maize and fish, acorns and pelts. But there are no gold, silver, or precious stones. And the storms are ferocious. ". . . Such a rainstorm came up that they could not carry an inch of sail." The ships became separated. "The sea was so high it was frightful to see. . . . " When they found each other, it was along a coast where "there are mountains which seem to reach the heavens, and the sea beats on them; sailing along close to land, it appears as though they would fall on the ships."

The pair of ships under Cabrillo reached Cape San Martin. Exhausted, Cabrillo decided to go back to La Posesión to restore himself and his men. But it was the end for him:

> While wintering at the Isla de Posesión, there passed from this present life, January 3, 1543, Juan Rodríguez Cabrillo, the captain of the ships, from a fall which he had in this island the previous time they were there, in which he broke an arm, close to the shoulder. He left as captain the chief pilot, who was one Bartolome Ferrelo, a native of the Levant, and strongly charged him at the time of his death not to fail to discover as much as possible of all that coast.

FERRELO TAKES OVER

His crew renamed the island for him: Isla de Juan Rodríguez. But like all the place names given on this expedition, it did not remain.

Ferrelo followed orders and sailed north, some believe as far as the coast of Oregon, but the exact point is not known beyond doubt. With Cabrillo gone, the expedition began to lose its driving force. Supplies were running out. There is even a change in the tone of the journal; more emotional, less understated than it was when Cabrillo commanded:

> ... The wind came from the southwest with great fury, the seas coming from many sides, which molested them very much or broke over the ships. As these had no covered decks, if the Lord had not aided them, they could not have escaped. . . . Considering themselves lost they commended themselves to our Señora de Guadalupe and made their vows. . . . At this hour the Mother of Our Lord succored them with the grace of Her Son, and a very strong rainstorm came up from the north which made them run before it towards the South with lower foresails all night and all the following day until sunset.

Ferrelo brought the ships back to Natividad, on April 14, 1543, after half a dozen close calls, including one over some reefs at the Isla de Juan Rodríguez, where "the sailors made a vow to go to their church stark naked and Our Lady saved them."

In retrospect, Cabrillo's voyage has been magnified as a great success. It was nothing of the sort, just a brave probe to the north, which found neither the passage to the Indies nor the fabled treasures of Cibola [the famous "Seven Cities" reputed to be filled with riches] or the island of the Amazon queen. The real riches of the land remained hidden. And if there was anything New Spain did not need when it was still digesting the vast Conquest of Mexico, it was more land. California was marginal, and as such it was given a low order of priority. Thus the land and its Indian inhabitants were not at this time seriously disturbed. There would be other explorations, and an English privateer named [Francis] Drake would land briefly on its coast. But the Spanish settlement of California would have to wait nearly 120 years.

1543 to 1606: The Europeans Vie for Control

═══╡ CHAPTER 5 ╞═══

TRISTÁN DE LUNA'S FAILED COLONY

WOODBURY LOWERY

In the following selection, Woodbury Lowery describes the hardships experienced by residents of Tristan de Luna y Arellano's colony. After establishing a base at Pensacola Bay, Florida, in 1559, the Spaniards sailed north and set up a colony at Nanipacna Bay. From the outset, the colonists suffered continually from lack of food and harsh weather. In addition, exploring parties sent by de Luna to look for food and arable lands returned with disappointing reports about barren, unoccupied terrain. According to Lowery, during the absence of one such party, the colonists were attacked by Indians and fled to Pensacola Bay. Once there, however, the colonists grew sicker and hungrier and began to turn on de Luna, who was determined to remain in Florida. Finally, the efforts of two Franciscan friars made de Luna realize his folly, and he and his colonists were reconciled. Nevertheless, shortly thereafter, the colonists abandoned the settlement. Woodbury Lowery was a Washington patent lawyer, historian, and author of *The Spanish Settlements Within the Present Limits of the United States, 1513–1561*, from which this excerpt was taken.

A landing [by Tristan de Luna y Arellano's fleet] was effected unopposed by the natives, who appeared to be few in number, and on the twenty-fourth of July 1559 Arellano sent a galleon back to Mexico with a report of the success which had so far attended his movements, the promise of a fertile and peopled country in the interior, and asking for more horses and supplies, that he might not be compelled to obtain food by force from the natives, whose good-will he desired to gain. It was his intention, he wrote, not to penetrate into the interior, but to colonise and fortify the port until the arrival of the supplies.

GENERAL DISASTER

Exploring parties, each accompanied by a monk, were sent in different directions along the shore and up the river into the interior; some of the stores were unloaded, but unfortunately, as it ultimately proved, the major part of the supplies, of which there were enough for one year, was left aboard the ships, and two vessels were equipped to carry the news to Spain, in one of which the ex-gunner, Fray Matheos, was to sail for home. But if the Indians had proved non-resisting, the winds now took up the gauntlet in defence of the plains and mountains where they were born. On the night of the 19th of September there came from the north a great tempest which lasted for twenty-four hours with constantly increasing violence. It shattered to pieces five ships, a galleon, and a bark, with great loss of life, among others that of the gunner-monk. It swept a caravel with its cargo into a grove of trees distant more than an arquebuse-shot from the shore, and besides the loss of the vessel carrying most of the provisions for the army the waters destroyed the greater part of the materials already landed. Indeed, so fierce and terrific was the storm and such the devastation it wrought, that, unable to account for it by natural means, it was attributed to evil spirits, and some of those on shore at the time averred that they had even seen the devils in the air.

In this extremity the colonists, awaiting the return of the explorers, lived upon what provisions were found in the stranded caravel, and Arellano determined that as soon as he should receive their report he would seek some place in the interior where the colonists could subsist, leaving what little food had escaped the general disaster for those who were to remain in the settlement he had established at the port. But after three weeks, the exploring parties returned with the discouraging news that the country was sterile and uninhabited. . . .

A SPIRIT OF DISCONTENT

During the prolonged absence of [another exploring party dispatched by Arellano,] sickness and famine had visited the eight hundred settlers who had remained at Nanipacna with the governor, and at last, all hope of the return of the [expedition] having been abandoned, [a] message [that explained that the colonists had returned to Pensacola Bay] was buried by [a] marked tree, the town was deserted, and the entire colony returned to the port. From here the provincial vicar, in company with the two remaining monks and a small party, had set sail for Havana, leaving the unfortunate colonists at Pensacola Bay quite without spiritual guidance. . . .

The hardships endured, the absence of active occupation, the failure to receive the promised supplies, were beginning to work the usual result, a spirit of discontent, stimulated, no doubt, by the escape from their enforced sufferings of those of their companions who had sailed away with the monks. For all were eager to depart except De Luna, who was determined on making a march to [the Indian town of] Coça [where the exploring party had gone]. The arrival of the messengers from Coça added fuel to the smouldering fire, and, won over by the malcontents, headed by the camp-master, who was averse to the Coça expedition and anxious to get away, they exaggerated the difficulties of the journey and the sterility of the Coça country. The governor stormed and fumed, ordered preparations to be made for the march, threatened the delinquents with the direst penalties, and even resorted to argument, but all to no purpose, for the discontented were in the majority and De Luna was unable to execute his threats. In the meantime the camp-master stole a march upon him by secretly recalling the major, who with his detachment presented himself at the port early in November after an absence of seven months. With him came the two monks, whose efforts among the natives, as far as they could know, had practically come to nothing, for only one Indian woman, who was in a dying condition, had asked for and received baptism at the hands of Fray Salaçar. These new arrivals also joined the ranks of the mutineers, while the governor, as determined as they, condemned them all to death as traitors, but could go no further, as practically the entire company was now set against him. Thus matters stood when there arrived from Mexico two vessels with supplies, sent out by the viceroy to the relief of the colony after hearing the story told by the provincial vicar.

The dissensions were prolonged throughout the winter of 1560–1561, the continued obstinacy of De Luna increasing the sense of irritation of his opponents, and five months elapsed in these vain recriminations. In Holy Week of 1561 a reconciliation was effected by the two monks, so creditable to all concerned, when one realises the acrimony and hatred which the quarrel prolonged through the scarcity and suffering of a winter season must have engendered, that even if the account be somewhat coloured by the natural predilection of the Dominican narrator for his own Order, its insertion here will be forgiven.

RECONCILIATION

Both Frays Salaçar and Anunciacion had laboured incessantly, in the spirit of their divine Master to secure peace, but with small result. At last, on Palm Sunday, Fray Anunciacion having confessed himself and the general, the camp-master, and the army being assembled to celebrate the solemnity of [according to Davila Padilla], so great a day, Father Anunciacion began to say mass.

> Having reached that place in the service where he was about to consume the most blessed Sacrament, he turned toward the people, with the holy Host in his hands, holding it upright above the paten. All were surprised at the novelty, waiting for what was to follow. The blessed father paused a little while, gazing devoutly at his God, his eyes shedding copious tears. In the midst of his tears, he lifted up his voice with the authority which God knows how to grant to him who serves Him, and called by his own name the Governor, who was kneeling in the place to which his rank entitled him. He rose at once and went in front of the altar, where he remained kneeling in expectation of what the blessed priest required of him. Again the blessed father paused a little, as if waiting to receive from God that which he was to say; and it was thus that God spoke through him.
>
> He said to the Governor, with a celestial grace: "Do you believe that this, which I hold in my unworthy hands, is the body of our Lord Jesus Christ, Son of the living God, who came from heaven to earth to redeem us all?" The Governor answered: "Yes, I believe it, sir." Again the monk said: "Do you believe that this same Lord is to come to judge the quick and the dead, and

that upon the good He will bestow glory, and upon the wicked eternal suffering in hell?" He also answered: "Yes, sir." At this second answer the Governor began to fear greatly, and his eyes filled with tears, for of a truth God had touched his heart; then the blessed father said to him: "If then you believe this, which every faithful Christian must believe, how is it that you are the cause of so many evils and sins, which we have suffered for five months, because you will not reconcile yourself with your captains to treat of a remedy for all this people, who for your sake have perished and are perishing, as I have often warned and implored you? If until now you have not hearkened unto men, listen to the Son of the Virgin, who speaks to you; and fear that same Son of God, who shall judge you. By this Lord, whom I hold here in my hands, I warn, I beseech and I command you, that you now do that which until now you have not wished to do, and if you do it, by command of the same Lord I promise you succour for all before three days have passed; and if you do it not, chastisement as by His hand."

Having thus spoken, he turned to the altar, and having finished the mass, went in and removed the sacred vestments. The Governor rose from the place he had taken at the foot of the altar when the blessed father called him, for he had remained there kneeling up to this point; and turning to the people, he said to them all with feeling and gentleness: "Gentlemen, you have seen what Fray Domingo has done, and have heard the strange words he spoke to me. I declare that if the fault is on my side, God has never willed that I should follow it, nor be the cause of so many evils. Until now and for the future for the love of God I forgive you all, gentlemen, from the bottom of my heart, and I beg you for the love of God that you forgive me the injuries I have done you and the evil you have suffered for my sake. I know that because of my sins God has chastised you all, and so I ask you all forgiveness as the aggressor and the guilty one." When he came to these words he could no longer contain his tears, but they burst forth with the intensity of his feeling, serving as ink, that that pardon might remain written and signed.

Then came the Camp-Master to the feet of the Governor, prostrating himself and begging his forgiveness with many tears. The General also shed tears, acknowledging himself as guilty. Then came the remaining captains, with the feelings and expressions of true love, whose fire had ignited not only the straw, but also the wood, which the devil had already cut from the mountain of mercy. When Father Fray Domingo de la Anunciacion related this event, thirty years after its occurrence," concludes the narrator, Fray Augustin Davila Padilla, historian of the Order in Mexico, "so fresh had he preserved those tears of the General and his captains, that the blessed old man shed them in abundance, giving thanks to God for His mercies, and moving even my heart, when I heard him.

FINAL SUCCOUR

The reconciled colonists began at once to devise a remedy for their miserable condition, but so demoralised were they in body and mind, so weak, famished, naked, and sick, that they were all day Monday without coming to a conclusion. Fortunately for them succour was near at hand.

On the arrival in Mexico of Fray Feria with the ill news of the condition of the Pensacola settlement, the viceroy, evidently dissatisfied with De Luna's conduct of affairs as represented to him by the provincial vicar, commissioned Angel de Villafañe to supersede Tristan de Luna and to carry succour to the colony. Four months before the incident just related Villafañe had sailed from Vera Cruz in his capacity of governor of Florida and with directions to occupy Santa Elena and trace the eastern coast. To the great joy of the colonists, his fleet, which had been delayed by adverse winds, now appeared in the harbour. He was attended by Fray Gregorio de Beteta, now on his second expedition to Florida, and by a number of friars who had come to convert the natives. With them came gifts for the two courageous monks, Frays Salaçar and Anunciacion, in whose hands the small quantity of flour left by the provincial vicar had not failed for the service of the mass, and for the comfort of the sick and dying through all this time,—not the least of several miraculous occurrences during De Luna's expedition. Villafañe offered to take all who chose to go with him to Santa Elena, and so universal was the desire to abandon the fateful bay, that Tristan de

Luna, finding himself entirely deserted, set sail for Havana with his servants, from whence he subsequently went to Spain and requested an investigation into his conduct. . . .

COLONISATION FAILURES

The attempts at colonisation on the Atlantic coast had miserably failed, because the soldier colonists, disdaining and ignoring all agricultural pursuits, had lived upon the sparse harvests of the natives. Nor was that all: driven to extremity by the failure of their supplies, the colonists had alienated them by stripping them of their winter stores, by compelling their enforced service, and by the exercise of those habits of harsh and brutal treatment which they had acquired in wars with the natives in other parts of the continent. And the very forces of nature had arrayed themselves on the side of the Indian. The sea and the wind and the winter seasons had battled to preserve intact the wigwam and hunting-ground of the savage. To the untrained vision of the mail-clad *caballero* the coast afforded no shelter for his armadas, and the unpeopled wastes gave no promise of agricultural returns. Small wonder then, that on the 23rd of September, [Spanish king] Philip II. declared that no further attempt should be made to colonise the eastern coast, convinced that there was no ground for fear that the French would take possession of it.

THE SPANISH ROUT THE FRENCH AND ESTABLISH SAN AGUSTÍN

IAN K. STEELE

Ian K. Steele is a history professor at the University of Western Ontario and the author of several books, including *Warpaths: Invasions of North America*, from which the following selection was excerpted. Steel explains how Spanish king Philip II engaged Pedro Menéndez de Avilés to rout the French colonizers from North America. In 1564, French navigator Jean Ribault established Fort Caroline on the east coast of Florida, which King Philip considered a threat to Spanish interests in the region. Soon thereafter, Menéndez and his squadron reached Fort Caroline and killed most of the French, including Ribault. Although the fort built by the Spanish at San Agustín in 1565 was soon destroyed by the Indians, a succession of wooden and stone forts was erected at the site over the next one-hundred years.

San Agustín represented a military model of a European invader's base. The Peace of Cateau-Cambrésis (1559) and the eruption of religiously oriented civil wars in France (1559–1589) had initially led Spain's Philip II to discount warnings that French Calvinist Huguenots were planning a settlement in North America, intended as both a refuge and a privateering base. Nonetheless, the first permanent Spanish settlement in

Ian K. Steele, *Warpaths: Invasions of North America*, New York: Oxford University Press, 1994. Copyright © 1994 by Oxford University Press. Reproduced by permission.

North America was initiated and sustained with support from the Spanish crown, anxious to defend its treasure fleets from these aggressive European rivals. The character of the venture would be affected by its founder and greatly influenced by missionary ambitions, but San Agustín would be established and maintained because it prevented European rivals from building privateering bases on that Florida coast.

THE FIRST FRENCH COLONY

French Admiral Gaspard de Coligny (1519–1572), a Huguenot leader who had invested in earlier American buccaneering and colonizing voyages, sent out a crown-approved preliminary expedition in the spring of 1562, under experienced navigators Jean Ribault (ca. 1520–1565) and an unknown renegade Portuguese pilot. Two ships carrying 150 men, including 75 soldiers, made a landfall in Saturiba Timucua territory near modern Jacksonville, Florida, and erected a stone column claiming the land for France. Ribault's party, with René Goulaine de Laudonnière as second in command, then coasted northward until they found the spacious harbor in Guale territory where [Spanish explorers Lucas Vasquez] Ayllón and Angel de Villafañe had tried to establish Santa Elena. Here they erected another stone column defining French claims and built a small wooden earthwork fort (Port Royal, South Carolina) and a house for the twenty-six men left behind as garrison. Losing their supplies in a fire, the garrison was sustained for a year only by food provided by friendly Guale. The Guale lived by hunting, fishing, and farming in villages of what would become coastal Georgia. Like those of their relatives, the Creek, each Guale village was led by a hereditary headman, or *mico*. Despite support from a friendly *mico*, the French fort failed because of its own brutal dissensions, and most survivors sailed for France in a makeshift sloop that the Guale were happy to help build. One Guilliaume Rouffi stayed behind, married into a Guale clan, and learned their language. In the spring of 1564, the Spanish burned the abandoned French fort and removed both the stone column and Rouffi, who would become useful to them as an interpreter.

FRENCH FAILURES

The first Huguenot settlement in Florida had self-destructed, but another soon followed. A court-approved French Huguenot fleet under Laudonnière, carrying three hundred sailors, soldiers, and colonists, arrived in June 1564. Like its predecessor, this expedition's landfall was in Saturiba territory near the St. John River, but this time a triangular Fort Caroline was built there (Jacksonville, Florida). Some two hundred men and two women stayed behind with Laudonnière when their fleet sailed for France late in July. This location was, even more obviously than Port Royal, a direct challenge to all Spanish shipping bound homeward from the Americas.

The French were initially well received by local Timucua chiefs who promptly drew them into intertribal warfare. These "settlers" did not plant crops, but traded for precious metals and built ships. Within six months, more than a third of the garrison had "stolen" newly built ships to raid the Spanish Caribbean. Their plunder, and their own capture, confirmed the worst Spanish suspicions about the purpose of the settlement. Internal dissent, outright war with the disillusioned neighboring Timucua, and resulting famine threatened Fort Caroline long before the Spanish could. Abandonment was narrowly averted by the arrival of Jean Ribault's large relief squadron of seven vessels carrying provisions and reinforcements of soldiers and colonists.

THE SPANISH RESPONSE

The Spanish response emerged gradually, but proved decisive. Pedro Menéndez de Avilés, a capable and experienced commander of the Indies fleets, was asked by Philip II to report on *La Florida* and on the best way to respond to the challenge of Ribault's first colony. Menéndez recommended three royally funded settlements on the Atlantic coast from Santa Elena north to Newfoundland, to be sustained by sugar and cattle production. However, in March 1565 he accepted the position of *adelantado*, meaning he would spend his own fortune in the area in return for extensive trade, land, and political privileges. Yet this was no mere *entrada*; settlement and defense had clear priority over exploration. Little was said of the native inhabitants, who apparently were to be drawn to the Spanish interest by missionaries. When Philip II heard, at the end of that month, of the second Huguenot colony, the newest Spanish venture to Florida was transformed. His terms for Menéndez became more generous, and the focus was on the very unpromising Florida Atlantic coast, which the Spanish had come to regard as worthless.

The expedition became a joint venture with the crown, with an urgent preliminary task of routing the French. Unknowingly, the parsimonious Philip II was launching a project that would, over the next three years, consume more than one-fifth of the entire military budget of his global empire.

Menéndez's five-vessel advance squadron, comprising less than a third of his total expedition, had failed in its race to beat Ribault to Florida. The Menéndez squadron reached the Fort Caroline area late in August 1565 with some eight hundred people aboard, including five hundred royal soldiers of varying levels of training, about two hundred sailors, and a hundred others, including colonists and the families of twenty-six soldiers. Menéndez's night attack drove off the four larger French ships anchored outside the river, but the five hundred French soldiers already landed prevented a direct attack on the fort. A Spanish force that could easily have overwhelmed the wintering French garrison, or prevailed if positioned between Fort Caroline and Ribault's reinforcements, could not challenge the reinforced and better protected French defenders. Menéndez withdrew southward some forty miles and went ashore to claim the country and formally establish the city of San Agustín.

Whatever he made of the European antics, the local Timucua village headman, Chief Seloy, saw nothing sinister in having the Spaniards fortify part of his village against the increasingly unwelcome French; Spaniards had come and gone before. Meanwhile, rival Timucua reported to the French at Fort Caroline of the Spanish landing and defenses. Fort Caroline was left with fewer than 250 defenders as Ribault launched a maritime attack intended to catch the Spanish unloading supplies. Acting on Timucua information and exploiting a prolonged storm that scattered Ribault's fleet and relaxed vigilance at Fort Caroline, Menéndez led his five hundred troops overland to attack the fort on its weaker landward side. One hundred and thirty-two Frenchmen were killed in the dawn attack, forty-five escaped, and about fifty Huguenot women and children were spared. The captured fort, well supplied and armed, became Fort San Mateo. Most of Ribault's fleet was wrecked along the shoreline south of San Agustín, and those who survived these disasters and attacks by local Ais tribesmen were forced to surrender unconditionally to Menéndez.

The ferocity of Reformation warfare was displayed clearly. The Spaniards summarily executed at least 111 prisoners as heretics and spared only 17. Another group, including Ribault, surrendered two weeks later and received similar treatment. Early in November, a remnant French group near Cape Canaveral, who had tried to fortify themselves with earthworks and salvaged ship cannon, fled to the woods at the approach of overwhelming Spanish force. About seventy-five surrendered when offered their lives, a civility Menéndez felt he could afford since the French threat had ended.

Menéndez and Philip II had been forced to establish a Spanish presence along the least fruitful Atlantic coast of Florida. A French settlement of any kind would have given legitimacy to armed French maritime presence throughout the Spanish Caribbean, for ships could be blown to strange places "by the stress of weather." Failed Spanish ventures had proven conclusively that the sandy soils and pine barrens of the south Atlantic coast could not sustain substantial Amerindian or European settlement, yet defense of the treasure fleets required a base at San Agustín rather than exploring the richer and more promising lands north of Santa Elena, or the great bay that Velázquez had found north of Cape Hatteras.

FRANCIS DRAKE CLAIMS CALIFORNIA FOR ENGLAND

HERBERT E. BOLTON AND EPHRAIM D. ADAMS

Herbert E. Bolton and Ephraim D. Adams explain in the following selection how English sailor Francis Drake claimed California for England in 1579. Drake had been plundering Spanish ships throughout portions of the Atlantic and Pacific Oceans and feared returning home through those regions. In consequence, Drake decided to return to England via India and Africa. Before setting out west over the Pacific, the English sailor headed North and eventually reached a place now referred to as Drake's Bay, which is just north of San Francisco. According to Bolton and Adams, the Englishman claimed the country for England and was knighted for his efforts by Queen Elizabeth upon his return home. Herbert E. Bolton was a history professor at the University of California, Berkeley, and author of several books on the Spanish borderlands. Ephraim D. Adams was a history professor at Stanford University.

B ut California was not forgotten. Soon after [Juan Rodríguez] Cabrillo's voyage [in 1542], Spanish sailors crossed the Pacific Ocean from Mexico and conquered the Philippine Islands. Now the California shore was often seen by sailors returning from Manila to Mexico, or looking for the strait, or for English "sea dogs," who robbed the Spanish ships of their gold and silver, and of their silks and spices.

Herbert E. Bolton and Ephraim D. Adams, *California's Story*, Boston, MA: Allyn and Bacon, 1922.

DRAKE CLAIMS CALIFORNIA FOR ENGLAND

The sea rover who most frightened the Spaniards was Francis Drake, a favorite of England's "Good Queen Bess" [Queen Elizabeth]. Several times he raided Spanish towns round the Gulf of Mexico. Later he boldly crossed the Atlantic with a fleet of ships and passed through the Straits of Magellan. All but one of his vessels turned back or were lost in a storm, but with his good ship *Pelican* he reached the Pacific Ocean. He now named his vessel the *Golden Hind*. Sailing up the coast he captured Spanish vessels, sacked towns, and robbed a pack train carrying gold along the shore. At one town he captured thirty-seven bars of gold, each one "of the fashion and bigness of a brickbat." At another place he cut the cables of a Spanish fleet anchored in the harbor. From a vessel which he pursued and captured on the sea he secured "jewels and precious stones, thirteen chests full of real plate [silver], four score pound weight of gold, and six and twenty tons of silver." Of course the Spaniards called him a pirate.

Drake feared to return through the Straits of Magellan, because of the storms there, and lest he be captured by the angered Spaniards. So he decided to cross the Pacific Ocean and return by way of India and Africa. Before crossing the ocean he sailed north and reached the coast of California, where he entered a harbor to repair the *Golden Hind*. The place where he stopped is still known as Drake's Bay. It can be seen on the map just north of San Francisco.

On the shore Drake found Indians living in houses of earth and poles. They spread the news of his arrival. Soon many more came from all the country round, bearing presents and making long speeches. They put a crown upon Drake's head, and wished to make him king, or "Great Hióh"—or at least so Drake thought. He accepted the crown, and claimed the country for England. Then he nailed to a post a plate bearing Queen Elizabeth's name, to warn the Spaniards to keep out. This was not the last time that strange happenings occurred on Drake's Bay. But nobody has ever yet found that plate.

From California Drake sailed away across the Pacific to Asia, and returned to England by way of the Cape of Good Hope. He had been round the world, a thing of which no other Englishman could boast. So great was his fame now that Queen Elizabeth visited the *Golden Hind*, and, standing on its deck, touched Drake's shoulder with a sword and made him a knight. By his bold voyage to California he had thus become *Sir* Francis Drake.

WHY THE ENGLISH SHOULD COLONIZE AMERICA

RICHARD HAKLUYT

Richard Hakluyt (the Elder) was an English lawyer who became interested in overseas colonization. In the following selection, excerpted from his 1585 tract "Inducements to the Liking of the Voyage Intended towards Virginia in 40. and 42. Degrees," Hakluyt sets down justifications for expanding English settlements in America. Most important of his justifications is the benefit of spreading Christianity to the Indians. Hakluyt also suggests that expanded colonization would increase England's honor, revenues, and power. In addition, he lists many of the valuable goods that could be obtained in the New World such as pearls, hides, wood, and marble. Hakluyt also explains that the colonies would be a good place to send England's unemployed youth so that they could work productively for the empire.

1. The glory of God by planting of religion among those infidels.
    2. The increase of the force of the Christians.
    3. The possibilitie of the inlarging of the dominions of the Queenes most excellent Majestie, and consequently of her honour, revenues, and of her power by this enterprise.
    4. An ample vent[1] in time to come of the Woollen clothes of England, especially those of the coursest sorts, to the mainte-

1. Market.

Richard Hakluyt, "Inducements to the Liking of the Voyage Intended Towards Virginia in 40. and 42. Degrees," *Envisioning America: English Plans for the Colonization of North America, 1580–1640,* edited by Peter C. Mancall, Boston, MA: Bedford Books of St. Martin's Press, 1995.

nance of our poore, that els sterve or become burdensome to the realme: and vent also of sundry our commodities upon the tract of that firme land, and possibly in other regions from the Northerne side of that maine.[2]

5. A great possibilitie of further discoveries of other regions from the North part of the same land by sea, and of unspeakable honor and benefit that may rise upon the same, by the trades to ensue in Japan, China, and Cathay,[3] &c.

6. By returne thence, this realme shall receive (by reason of the situation of the climate, and by reason of the excellent soile) Oade,[4] Oile, Wines, Hops, Salt, and most or all the commodities that we receive from the best parts of Europe, and we shall receive the same better cheape, than now we receive them, as we may use the matter.

7. Receiving the same thence, the navie, the humane strength of this realme, our merchants and their goods shal not be subject to arrest of ancient enemies & doubtfull friends, as of late yeeres they have beene.

8. If our nation do not make any conquest there, but only use trafficke and change of commodities, yet by meane the countrey is not very mightie, but divided into pety kingdoms, they shall not dare to offer us any great annoy, but such as we may easily revenge with sufficient chastisement to the unarmed people there.

9. Whatsoever commodities we receive by the Steelyard merchants, or by our owne merchants from Eastland,[5] be it Flaxe, Hempe, Pitch, Tarre, Masts, Clap-boord,[6] Wainscot,[7] or such like; the like good may we receive from the North and Northeast part of that countrey neere unto Cape Briton,[8] in returne for our course Woollen clothes, Flanels and Rugges fit for those colder regions.

PROTECTING TRADE

10. The passage to and fro, is thorow the maine Ocean sea, so as we are not in danger of any enemies coast.

11. In the voyage, we are not to crosse the burnt Zone,[9] nor to passe thorow frozen seas encombred with ice and fogs, but in

2. Mainland.   3. Northern China.   4. Oade is woad, a blue dye-stuff produced from powdered and fermented leaves of *Isatis tinctoria,* a plant sometimes called garden woad or dyer's weed.   5. The lands bordering on the Baltic Sea.   6. A narrow board of split oak, imported into England from northern Germany and used for making barrel staves. 7. A superior quality of foreign oak imported into England from Russia, Germany, and Holland and chiefly used for fine paneling.   8. Island east of present-day Nova Scotia. 9. Tropics.

temperate climate at all times of the yeere: and it requireth not, as the East Indie voiage doth, the taking in of water in divers places, by reason that it is to be sailed in five or six weeks: and by the shortnesse, the merchant may yeerely make two returnes (a factory once being erected there) a matter in trade of great moment.[10]

12. In this trade by the way in our passe to and fro, we have in tempests and other haps, all the ports of Ireland to our aid, and no neere coast of any enemy.

13. By this ordinary trade we may annoy the enemies to Ireland, and succour the Queenes Majesties friends there, and in time we may from Virginia yeeld them whatsoever commoditie they now receive from the Spaniard; and so the Spaniards shall want the ordinary victual[11] that heertofore they received yeerely from thence, and so they shall not continue trade, nor fall so aptly in practise against this government, as now by their trade thither[12] they may.

14. We shall, as it is thought, enjoy in this voyage, either some small Islands to settle on, or some one place or other on the firme land to fortifie for the saftie of our ships, our men, and our goods, the like whereof we have not in any forren place of our trafficke,[13] in which respect we may be in degree of more safetie, and more quiet.

15. The great plentie of Buffe[14] hides, and of many other sundry kinds of hides there now presently to be had, the trade of Whale and Seale fishing, and of divers other fishings in the great rivers, great bayes, and seas there, shall presently defray the charge in good part or in all of the first enterprise, and so we shall be in better case than our men were in Russia, where many yeeres were spent, and great summes of money consumed, before gaine was found.

16. The great broad rivers of that maine that we are to enter into so many leagues navigable or portable into the maine land, lying so long a tract with so excellent and so fertile a soile on both sides, doe seeme to promise all things that the life of man doth require, and whatsoever men may wish, that are to plant upon the same, or to trafficke in the same.

17. And whatsoever notable commoditie the soile within or without doth yeeld in so long a tract that is to be carried out

---

10. Of great importance.   11. Food or provisions.   12. Until then.   13. Trade or commerce.   14. Buffalo or other large species of wild ox.

from thence to England, the same rivers so great and deepe, do yeeld no small benefit for the sure, safe, easie and cheape cariage of the same to shipboord, be it of great bulke or of great weight.

THE GREAT RIVERS

18. And in like sort whatsoever commoditie of England the Inland people there shall need, the same rivers doe worke the like effect in benefit for the incariage of the same, aptly, easily, and cheaply.

19. If we find the countrey populous, and desirous to expel us, and injuriously to offend us, that seeke but just and lawful trafficke, then by reason that we are lords of navigation, and they not so, we are the better able to defend our selves by reason of those great rivers, & to annoy them in many places.

20. Where there be many petie kings or lords planted on the rivers sides, and by all likelihood mainteine the frontiers of their severall territories by warres, we may by the aide of this river joine with this king heere, or with that king there, at our pleasure, and may so with a few men be revenged of any wrong offered by any of them; or may, if we will proceed with extremitie,[15] conquer, fortifie, and plant in soiles most sweet, most pleasant, most strong, and most fertile, and in the end bring them all in subjection and to civilitie.

21. The knowen abundance of Fresh fish in the rivers, and the knowen plentie of Fish on the sea coast there, may assure us of sufficient victuall in spight of the people, if we will use salt and industrie.

22. The knowen plentie and varietie of Flesh, of divers kinds of beasts at land there, may seeme to say to us, that we may cheaply victuall our navies to England for our returnes, which benefit every where is not found of merchants.

23. The practise of the people of the East Indies, when the Portugals came thither first, was to cut from the Portugals their lading of Spice: and heereby they thought to overthrow their purposed trade. If these people shall practise the like, by not suffering[16] us to have any commoditie of theirs without conquest, (which requireth some time) yet may we mainteine our first voyage thither, till our purpose come to effect, by the seafishing on the coasts there, and by dragging for pearles, which are said to be on those parts; and by returne of those commodi-

15. Extreme intensity or violence.   16. Allowing, giving permission, tolerating.

ties, the charges in part shall be defraied: which is a matter of consideration in enterprises of charge.

24. If this realme shall abound too too much with youth, in the mines there of Golde, (as that of Chisca and Saguenay)[17] of Silver, Copper, Yron, &c. may be an imployment to the benefit of this realme; in tilling of the rich soile there for graine, and in planting of Vines there for Wine; or dressing of those Vines which grow there naturally in great abundance, Olives for Oile; Orenge trees, Limons, Figs and Almonds for fruit; Oad, Saffron, and Madder[18] for Diers; Hoppes for Brewers; Hempe, Flaxe; and in many such other things, by imploiment of the soile, our people void of sufficient trades, may be honestly imploied, that els may become hurtfull at home.

25. The navigating of the seas in the voyage, and of the great rivers there, will breed many Mariners for service, and mainteine much navigation.

26. The number of raw Hides there of divers kindes of beasts, if we shall possesse some Island there, or settle on the firme, may presently imploy many of our idle people in divers severall dressings of the same, and so we may returne them to the people that can not dresse them so well; or into this realm, where the same are good merchandize; or to Flanders,[19] &c. which present gaine at the first, raiseth great incouragement presently to the enterprise.

NATURAL RESOURCES

27. Since great waste Woods be there, of Oake, Cedar, Pine, Wallnuts, and sundry other sorts, many of our waste people may be imployed in making of Ships, Hoies, Busses[20] and Boats; and in making of Rozen, Pitch and Tarre, the trees naturall for the same, being certeinly knowen to be neere Cape Briton and the Bay of Menan,[21] and in many other places there about.

28. If mines of white or gray marble, Jet, or other rich stone be found there, our idle people may be imployed in the mines of the same, and in preparing the same to shape, and so shaped, they may be caried into this realm as good balast[22] for our ships, and after serve for noble buildings.

17. The Saguenay is a river in northeastern Canada flowing into the St. Lawrence River. 18. A herbaceous climbing plant cultivated for the dye obtained from it.   19. Present-day Belgium.   20. Hoys were small boats often used to carry people and goods along the coast. Busses were two- or three-masted fishing boats.   21. Perhaps present-day Grand Manan Channel, off the southwest coast of New Brunswick, Canada.   22. Ballast, heavy material placed in the hold of a ship to prevent capsizing when in motion.

29. Sugar-canes may be planted as well as they are now in the South of Spaine, and besides the imploiment of our idle people, we may receive the commodity cheaper, and not inrich infidels or our doubtful friends, of whom now we receive that commoditie.

30. The daily great increase of Woolles in Spaine, and the like in the West Indies, and the great imploiment of the same into Cloth in both places, may moove us to endevour, for vent of our Cloth, new discoveries of peopled regions, where hope of sale may arise; otherwise in short time many inconveniences may possibly ensue.

31. This land that we purpose to direct our course to, lying in part in the 40 degree of latitude, being in like heat as Lisbone in Portugall doth, and in the more Southerly part as the most Southerly coast of Spaine doth, may by our diligence yeeld unto us besides Wines and Oiles and Sugars, Orenges, Limons, Figs, Resings,[23] Almonds, Pomegranates, Rice, Rawsilks such as come from Granada, and divers commodities for Diers, as Anile and Cochenillio,[24] and sundry other colours and materials. Moreover, we shall not onely receive many precious commodities besides from thence, but also shal in time finde ample vent of the labour of our poore people at home, by sale of Hats, Bonets, Knives, Fish-hooks, Copper kettles, Beads, Looking-glasses, Bugles, & a thousand kinds of other wrought wares, that in short time may be brought in use among the people of that countrey, to the great reliefe of the multitude of our poore people, and to the woonderfull enriching of this realme. And in time, such league & entercourse may arise betweene our Stapling[25] seats there, and other ports of our Northern America, and of the Islands of the same, that incredible things, and by few as yet dreamed of, may speedily follow, tending to the impeachment of our mightie enemies, and to the common good of this noble government.

The ends of this voyage are these:

1. To plant Christian religion.
2. To trafficke.[26]
3. To conquer.

Or, to doe all three.

23. Raisins.   24. Anil is the indigo shrub or dye. Cochineal is a dyestuff consisting of the dried bodies of *Coccus cacti*, an insect found on several species of cactus; it produces a brilliant scarlet dye.   25. Referring to a town or place, appointed by royal authority, where a group of merchants had exclusive rights to buy and export commodities. 26. To carry on trade.

JOHN WHITE'S LOST COLONY

DISCOVERING U.S. HISTORY

In the following selection, *DISCovering U.S. History* recounts the misfortunes experienced by the first English colonists to America. At the urging of Sir Walter Raleigh, England's first colony was established on Roanoke Island—which is located off the coast of modern-day North Carolina—in 1585. This first colony, led by Ralph Lane, failed largely due to conflicts with the Indians and the colonists' refusal to learn the food-gathering practices necessary to survive. In the spring of 1586, the colonists returned to England.

Raleigh was determined to colonize North America, and in 1587 he arranged for a new colony headed by John White, originally a member of Lane's group. White set up a colony on Roanoke Island, and, shortly thereafter, his daughter gave birth to the first English child ever born in America. Unfortunately, later that year, White had to return to England to check on supplies for the colony. After several maddening delays, White returned to the colony in 1590 only to discover that the colony had vanished. *DISCovering U.S. History* is a history series published by the Gale Group and made available by the publisher on its History Resource Center database.

John White was a pivotal figure in establishing England's first colony in America, a settlement on Roanoke Island, off the coast of modern-day North Carolina. As a painter and cartographer on the first of two colonization expeditions sponsored by England's Sir Walter Raleigh, White provided documentation of the appearance of the Native American peoples that the Englishmen encountered. His detailed illustrations remain important tools for historians engaged in the study of Indian culture. On the second of the Raleigh-sponsored voyages to the New World, White was placed in charge of the would-be colonizers. In 1587 the colonists arrived at Roanoke and set about carving out a permanent place for themselves in the unfamiliar North American wilderness. White returned to England for supplies, but when he returned to America in 1590, the colony that he had left behind had mysteriously vanished.

SIR WALTER RALEIGH ORGANIZES THE COLONIZATION EFFORT

Little is known of John White's life prior to his voyages to the New World. Only after Sir Walter Raleigh became intrigued by reports of the New World did White's name begin to appear in the historical accounts of the day. By 1585 Raleigh had become convinced that an English settlement could be established in America, and plans for a colonization expedition were made. On April 9, 1585, Raleigh's fleet embarked for the New World.

The fleet reached America, but its main supply vessel was dashed against the rocks of the Outer Banks that shielded Roanoke Island from the Atlantic Ocean. By September the colony, led by Captain Ralph Lane, had settled on the island at the invitation of Wingina, a chief of the Roanoke tribe, one of several Indian tribes in the region. Once the colony had been established, John White was free to indulge his interest in artwork and painting, and he made many illustrations of the strange plants and animals that surrounded him. He is perhaps best known, however, for his portraits of the Native American peoples that he and the other colonists encountered. White's illustrations indicate that these Indians were tall and sturdy, with strong facial features and jet-black hair. He also documented their colorful appearance, and White's portraits indicated that the coastal Indians adorned themselves in a wide array of animal hides, tattoos, and necklaces and bracelets festooned with feathers, shells, pearls, and animal claws.

The loss of the main supply ship, meanwhile, proved to be a blow from which the colonists could not recover. As the colonists waited for another supply vessel to arrive from England, they became increasingly dependent on area Indians for food. Still, they showed only tepid enthusiasm for learning about the food-gathering practices of the Native Americans, and the Roanokes became increasingly resentful. Tensions between the two groups were exacerbated during the winter of 1585 and the spring of 1586, and bloodshed finally erupted. Wingina was killed in the battle, and the surviving Roanokes fled. A short time later, the hungry colonists learned that a fleet under the command of Englishman Sir Francis Drake was in the area. Lane informed Drake of the colony's plight, and the explorer agreed to provide the colony with food, clothing, and equipment. A sudden storm rose up, however, and most of the supplies were lost to the watery depths. Lane subsequently accepted Drake's offer to return the colony to England.

THE SECOND COLONY

Upon Lane's return, Raleigh remained adamant about establishing a colony on Roanoke Island. He arranged for a new colonization effort under the governorship of White, and on May 8, 1587, the expedition set out from England. Accompanying White was his daughter Eleanor and his son-in-law Ananias Dare.

The colony had hoped to settle at Chesapeake Bay, but the commander of the fleet was anxious to rid himself of the colonizers so that he could begin privateering. White's group of 117 settlers were forced to land on Roanoke Island and make plans to relocate to Chesapeake Bay in the spring of 1587. But even though the hot-tempered Lane was not a part of this second colonization effort, relations with area Indians did not improve. After one colonist was killed by the remnants of the Roanoke tribe, White ordered an ambush of a nearby Indian settlement. Only after the attack did the Englishmen realize that they had mistakenly attacked innocent Indians from the Croatoan tribe.

On August 18, 1587, John White's daughter, Eleanor Dare, gave birth to a baby girl named Virginia Dare. The infant was the first English child ever born in America. White exulted in the birth of his grandchild, but his happiness was short-lived.

The colony had decided that a representative should return to England in one of their smaller vessels in order to assure that needed supplies scheduled for delivery the following year would be sent. The colonists finally decided that White himself should go, but the governor objected. White feared that the people of England would judge him a coward for leaving the colony, where he had hoped to spend the rest of his life. Finally, though, they convinced him to go.

White's voyage back to England was fraught with peril, but he eventually made it back. He met with Raleigh, who made arrangements for a supply fleet to set sail in the spring of 1588. Prior to departure, however, Queen Elizabeth ordered a ban on transatlantic travel and ordered the fleet into military duty. Spain was preparing to invade England, and it was determined that Raleigh's vessels could not be spared.

Despite this turn of events, however, Raleigh managed to outfit two small vessels for the colonies, and in late April 1588 the ships set out for America. They were intercepted by French pirates, however, and White was badly wounded in the vicious fight. Raleigh's ships were forced to retreat to England.

THE LOST COLONY

White recovered from his injuries, but he despaired about the colony's well-being. The mighty Spanish Armada was defeated in 1588, but it was not until 1590 that White was able to gain passage back to the New World. He hopped a ride aboard the *Hopewell*, a warship charged with raiding Spanish trade vessels in the Caribbean, but the ship eventually made its way north, and a small party headed by White landed at the site of the Roanoke colony in August 1590. White was stunned to discover that the colony had vanished. He could find no sign of struggle, and no bodies were found. But everyone had vanished, and the houses that had been constructed by the colonists had been neatly removed. White did find three chests of his belongings, which the settlers had apparently buried. He speculated that Indians might have gone through the chests, for his things were "spoiled and broken and my books torn from their covers . . . some of my pictures and maps rotten and spoiled with rain, and my armor almost eaten through with rust."

The only clue to the disappearance of the Roanoke colony was a single word—CROATOAN—that had been carved into a nearby tree. Some speculated that the colony had taken refuge with the Croatoan tribe, or that they had relocated to an island in the vicinity known by that name. But no further clue as to the disappearance of the colony was ever found, and their fate remains a mystery.

Disheartened, White returned to England. It is believed that he soon moved to Ireland, where he spent the last years of his life. He is thought to have died there in 1593.

THE ROANOKE MYSTERY

JOHN WHITE

John White was an artist, writer, and the leader of an English colony established at Roanoke Island in 1587. In the following selection, excerpted from his diary, White describes what he found when he returned to the colony in 1590 from a trip to England. According to White, all of the colonists had vanished and their belongings had been despoiled. The only clue as to their fate were the letters "CROATOAN" carved into a tree. Based on this evidence, White assumed that the colonists had gone to live with the friendly Croatoan Indians. However, the colonists were never heard from again.

T he next morning being the 17th of August, 1590, our boats and company were prepared again to go up to Roanoke, North Carolina. . . . The admiral's boat was halfway toward the shore, when Captain Spicer put off from his ship. The Admiral's boat first passed the breach, but not without some danger of sinking, for we had a sea break into our boat which filled us half full of water, but by the will of God and careful steerage of Captain Cooke we came safe ashore, saving only that our furniture, victuals, match and powder were much wet and spoiled. For at this time the wind blew at Northeast and direct into the harbour so great a gale, that the Sea broke extremely on the bar, and the tide went very forcibly at the entrance. By that time our admiral's boat was hauled ashore, and most of our things taken out to dry, Captain Spicer came to the entrance of the breach with his mast standing up, and was half

John White, "John White's Diary," *America Firsthand, Volume 1, From Settlement to Reconstruction*, edited by Robert Marcus and David Burner, New York: St. Martin's Press, 1995.

passed over, but by the rash and indiscreet steerage of Ralph Skinner his Master's mate, a very dangerous Sea broke into their boat and overset them quite. . . . They were eleven in all, and seven of the chiefest were drowned. . . . This mischance did so much discomfort the sailors, that they were all of one mind not to go any further to seek the planters. But in the end by the commandment and persuasion of me and Captain Cooke, they prepared the boats. And seeing the Captain and me so resolute, they seemed much more willing.

LOCATING THE COLONY

Our boats and all things fitted again, we put off from Hatorask, being the number of nineteen persons in both boats: but before we could get to the place, where our planters were left, it was so exceedingly dark, that we overshot the place a quarter of a mile. There we spied towards the North end of the island the light of a great fire through the woods, to the which we presently rowed. When we came right over against it, we let fall our grapnel near the shore, and sounded with a trumpet a call, and afterwards many familiar English tunes of songs, and called to them friendly; but we had no answer. We therefore landed at day-break, and coming to the fire, we found the grass and sundry rotten trees burning about the place. From hence we went through the woods to that part of the island directly over against Dasamongwepeuk, and from thence we returned by the water side, round about the North point of the island, until we came to the place where I left our Colony in the year 1587.

In all this way we saw in the sand the print of the savages' feet of two or three sort trodden the night, and as we entered up the sandy bank upon a tree, in the very brow thereof were curiously carved these fair Roman letters C R O: which letters presently we knew to signify the place, where I should find the planters seated, according to a secret token agreed upon between them and me at my last departure from them, which was, that in any ways they should not fail to write or carve on the trees or posts of the doors the name of the place where they should be seated; for at my coming away they were prepared to remove from Roanoke 50 miles into the main. Therefore at my departure from them in A.D. 1587 I willed them, that if they should happen to be distressed in any of those places, that then they should carve over the letters or name, a Cross ✠ in this form, but we found no such sign of distress.

REMNANTS OF A LOST COLONY

And having well considered of this, we passed toward the place where they were left in sundry houses, but we found the houses taken down, and the place very strongly enclosed with a high palisade of great trees, with continues and flankers very Fort-like, and one of the chief trees or posts at the right side of the entrance had the bark taken off, and 5 foot from the ground in fair Capital letters was graven CROATOAN without any cross or sign of distress. This done, we entered into the palisade, where we found many bars of iron, two pigs of lead, four iron fowlers, iron sacker-shot, and such like heavy things, thrown here and there, almost overgrown with grass and weeds. From thence we went along by the water side, towards the point of the Creek to see if we could find any of their boats or pinnace, but we could perceive no sign of them, nor any of the last falkons and small ordinance which were left with them, at my departure from them.

At our return from the Creek, some of our sailors meeting us, told us that they had found where divers chests had been hidden, and long since dug up again and broken up, and much of the goods in them spoiled and scattered about, but nothing left, of such things as the Savages knew any use of, undefaced. Presently Captain Cooke and I went to the place, which was in the end of an old trench, made two years past by Captain Amadas: where we found five chests, that had been carefully hidden of the Planters, and of the same chests three were my own, and about the place many of my things spoiled and broken, and my books torn from the covers, the frames of some of my pictures and maps rotten and spoiled with rain, and my armor almost eaten through with rust. This could be no other but the deed of the Savages our enemies at Dasamongwepeuk, who had watched the departure of our men to Croatoan; and as soon as they were departed, dug up every place where they suspected any thing to be buried. But although it much grieved me to see such spoil of my goods, yet on the other side I greatly joyed that I had safely found a certain token of their safe being at Croatoan, which is the place where . . . the savages of the island [are] our friends.

THE CAROLINA ALGONQUIAN

THOMAS HARRIOT

In the following selection, scientist Thomas Harriot, a member of John White's colony, describes the Algonquian who lived in what is now North Carolina (which the English called Virginia). The most notable edition of Harriot's promotional report was the folio edition of 1590, which included a series of his engravings based on the paintings of John White.

According to Harriot, the Algonquian lived in small seaside towns containing ten to thirty houses made from poles. Harriot characterizes the Algonquian as subtle and devious warriors who fought with one another and with the colonists. They believed in several gods and also in concepts similar to Heaven and Hell. The Algonquian also believed that the dead could rise again to serve as examples to the living. Harriot thought that these religious beliefs helped make the Algonquian obedient and good.

I t resteth[1] I speake a word or two of the naturall inhabitants [the Carolina Algonquian], their natures and maners, leaving large discourse thereof until time more convenient hereafter: nowe onely so farre foorth, as that you may know, how that they in respect of troubling our inhabiting and planting, are

---

1. Remains to be done.

Thomas Harriot, "A Briefe and True Report of the New Found Land of Virginia," *Envisioning America: English Plans for the Colonization of North America, 1580–1640*, edited by Peter C. Mancall, Boston, MA: Bedford Books of St. Martin's Press, 1995.

not to be feared, but that they shall have cause both to feare and love us, that shall inhabite with them.

ALGONQUIAN TOWNS

They are a people clothed with loose mantles made of deere skinnes, and aprons of the same round about their middles, all els naked, of such a difference of statures onely as wee in England, having no edge tooles or weapons of yron or steele to offend us withall, neither knowe they how to make any: those weapons that they have, are onely bowes made of Witch-hazle, and arrowes of reedes, flat edged truncheons also of wood about a yard long, neither have they any thing to defend themselves but targets[2] made of barkes, and some armours made of sticks wickered together with thread.

Their townes are but small, and neere the Sea coast but fewe, some contayning but tenne or twelve houses; some 20. the greatest that we have seene hath bene but of 30. houses: if they bee walled, it is onely done with barkes of trees made fast to stakes, or els with poles onely fixed upright, and close one by another.

Their houses are made of small poles, made fast at the tops in round forme after the maner as is used in many arbories in our gardens of England, in most townes covered with barkes, and in some with artificiall mats made of long rushes, from the tops of the houses downe to the ground. The length of them is commonly double to the breadth, in some places they are but 12. and 16. yards long, and in other some we have seene of foure and twentie.

In some places of the Countrey, one onely towne belongeth to the government of a Wiroans[3] or chiefe Lord, in other some two or three, in some sixe, eight, and more: the greatest Wiroans that yet wee had dealing with, had but eighteene townes in his government, and able to make not above seven or eight hundreth fighting men at the most. The language of every government is different from any other, and the further they are distant, the greater is the difference.

Their maner of warres amongst themselves is either by sudden surprising one an other most commonly about the dawning of the day, or moone-light, or els by ambushes, or some subtile devises. Set battels are very rare, except it fall out where

2. Light, round shields.   3. A chief of Virginia Indians.

there are many trees, where either part may have some hope of defence, after the delivery of every arrow, in leaping behind some or other.

If there fall out any warres betweene us and them, what their fight is likely to bee, wee having advantages against them so many maner of wayes, as by our discipline, our strange weapons and devises else, especially Ordinance[4] great and small, it may easily bee imagined: by the experience wee have had in some places, the turning up of their heeles against us in running away was their best defence.

In respect of us they are a people poore, and for want of skill and judgement in the knowledge and use of our things, doe esteeme our trifles before things of greater value: Notwithstanding, in their proper maner (considering the want of such meanes as we have), they seeme very ingenious. For although they have no such tooles, nor any such crafts, Sciences and Artes as wee, yet in those things they doe, they shew excellence of wit. And by how much they upon due consideration shall finde our maner of knowledges and crafts to exceede theirs in perfection, and speede for doing or execution, by so much the more is it probable that they should desire our friendship and love, and have the greater respect for pleasing and obeying us. Whereby may bee hoped, if meanes of good government be used, that they may in short time bee brought to civilitie, and the imbracing of true Religion.

ALGONQUIAN RELIGION

Some religion they have already, which although it be farre from the trueth, yet being as it is, there is hope it may be the easier and sooner reformed.

They beleeve that there are many gods, which they call Mantoac, but of different sorts & degrees, one onely chiefe and great God, which hath bene from all eternitie. Who, as they affirme, when hee purposed to make the world, made first other gods of a principall order, to be as meanes and instruments to be used in the creation and government to follow, and after the Sunne, moone, and starres as pettie gods, and the instruments of the other order more principal. First (they say) were made waters, out of which by the gods was made all diversitie of creatures that are visible or invisible.

4. Display of military force.

For mankinde they say a woman was made first, which by the working of one of the gods, conceived and brought foorth children: And in such sort they say they had their beginning. But how many yeeres or ages have passed since, they say they can make no relation, having no letters nor other such meanes as we to keepe Records of the particularities of times past, but onely tradition from father to sonne.

They thinke that all the gods are of humane shape, and therefore they represent them by images in the formes of men, which they call Kewasowok, one alone is called Kewas: them they place in houses appropriate or temples, which they call Machicomuck, where they worship, pray, sing, and make many times offring unto them. In some Machicomuck we have seene but one Kewas, in some two, and in other some three. The common sort thinke them to be also gods.

They beleeve also the immortalitie of the soule, that after this life as soone as the soule is departed from the body, according to the workes it hath done, it is either caried to heaven the habitacle[5] of gods, there to enjoy perpetuall blisse and happinesse, or els to a great pitte or hole, which they thinke to be in the furthest parts of their part of the world toward the Sunne set, there to burne continually: the place they call Popogusso.

LIFE AFTER DEATH

For the confirmation of this opinion, they tolde me two stories of two men that had bene lately dead and revived againe, the one happened but few yeeres before our comming into the Countrey of a wicked man, which having bene dead and buried, the next day the earth of the grave being seene to move, was taken up againe, who made declaration where his soule had bene, that is to say, very neere entring into Popogusso, had not one of the gods saved him, and gave him leave to returne againe, and teach his friends what they should do to avoyd that terrible place of torment. The other happened in the same yeere we were there, but in a towne that was 60. miles from us, and it was told me for strange newes, that one being dead, buried, and taken up againe as the first, shewed that although his body had lien dead in the grave, yet his soule was alive, & had travailed farre in a long broad way, on both sides whereof grew most delicate and pleasant trees, bearing more rare and excellent fruits,

5. Dwelling place.

then ever hee had seene before, or was able to expresse, and at length came to most brave and fair houses, neere which he met his father that had bene dead before, who gave him great charge to goe backe againe, and shew his friendes what good they were to doe to enjoy the pleasures of that place, which when he had done he should after come againe.

What subtiltie soever be in the Wiroances and priestes, this opinion worketh so much in many of the common and simple sort of people, that it maketh them have great respect to their Governours, and also great care what they doe, to avoyd torment after death, and to enjoy blisse, although notwithstanding there is punishment ordeined for malefactours,[6] as stealers, whoremongers, and other sorts of wicked doers, some punished with death, some with forfeitures,[7] some with beating, according to the greatnesse of the facts.

And this is the summe of their Religion, which I learned by having speciall familiaritie with some of their priests. Wherein they were not so sure grounded, nor gave such credite to their traditions and stories, but through conversing with us they were brought into great doubts of their owne, and no small admiration of ours, with earnest desire in many, to learne more then wee had meanes for want of perfect utterance in their language to expresse.

6. Evildoers.   7. Deprivation of an estate after committing a crime.

JUAN DE OÑATE'S COLONY AND THE PUEBLO

JAY MILLER

Jay Miller is the author of several books on Indian subjects. In the following selection, Miller tells about the systematic brutality of Juan de Oñate and his New Mexico colonists. According to Miller, in 1598, Oñate was granted all of present-day New Mexico by the Spanish king, and he established a colony in the Tewa Indian Village of San Juan. In the beginning, the San Juan Indians were not too concerned with having to move out of their pueblos—they were more attached to the land than to their dwellings. Besides, the Tewas could simply join others of their people who lived across the Rio Grande River. However, relations between the Indians and the colonists quickly deteriorated. For one thing, the Spanish missionaries forcibly converted the Indians to Catholicism. For another, the colonists quickly depleted the Tewa's resources, especially their food. Miller explains that Oñate's colonists viciously suppressed any resistance to these outrages through torture, murder, and rape.

I n 1598, all of present-day New Mexico was granted to Juan de Oñate to found a permanent colony at his own expense, as was the common practice of the Spanish. This colony included 400 men (130 of them with families), many native Mexican servants, and 83 oxcarts, accompanied by over 7,000 horses, plus cattle, sheep, and goats. The Pueblos had no hope of opposing such an assemblage.

Jay Miller, "The Southwest and Coastal California," *The Native Americans: An Illustrated History*, edited by Betty Ballantine and Ian Ballantine, Atlanta, GA: Turner Publishing, Inc., 1993.

SAN JUAN CONVERTED TO SAN GABRIEL

Nevertheless, Oñate avoided the central Rio Grande, already brutalized by [Francisco de] Coronado and his successors, and instead made his headquarters in the upper valley to the north. Forced to accept the inevitable, the native priests of the pueblo called San Juan agreed to yield a neighborhood of the Tewa town to the Spanish. At the urging of the priests, all the Indians moved out of that neighborhood. The Spanish settled in, christening their new home San Gabriel. In occupying the pueblo, the Spanish enlarged the rooms, added windows, and rearranged the entrances, both for defense—a factor they were always aware of—and to suit their own architectural tastes. A small church was also built, and consecrated to San Miguel. Meanwhile, the displacement of the native population concentrated its members even closer together, increasing the authority of the priests, and making their own defensive actions that much easier to organize.

The Tewa people, then as now, were divided into Summer and Winter moieties. In 1598, these halves were separated by the Rio Grande. The west side, which later became the Spanish San Gabriel, was called Yunge (Mockingbird Place), and it was occupied by the Summer moiety. The east side, called Okeh, was home to the Winter moiety. The entire town was governed by the leaders of each half during its appropriate season, summer or winter, and both halves were integrated by an interlocking hierarchy of priests who combined in their persons both civil authority and religious leadership. Indeed, the two were inseparable.

Each Pueblo town was tightly organized under a series of overlapping priesthoods. Pueblo priests controlled the affairs of each community, conducted elaborate masked rituals dedicated to supernatural beings called *kachinas*, and passed on generations of ecological wisdom that enabled farmers to thrive in an arid environment. The factor that controlled this concentration of power in the priesthood was the division into Summer and Winter moieties. Each half had to perform well for all to benefit, for if either half performed badly, all would suffer. So seeing the world from another point of view, recognizing the needs of others, was built into the Pueblo system of thinking and belief.

The Tewas, like other Pueblo peoples, were profoundly rooted in their land, through the everyday practicalities of their farming economy as well as the spiritual dimensions that pervaded all existence. Every stage of the planting and harvesting of the fields was regulated by the priests and the ritual calendar. The territory surrounding the town was seen as a series of spiritually significent concentric rings that served to direct and focus the life flow into and out of the center of the community. At the margins of the Tewa lands lay a ring of sacred mountains and hills; closer in was a circle of shrines that the Tewa people had constructed; and finally came the town's interior plazas and kivas, where the principal dances and rites were conducted.

When the site of San Juan was developed, over six hundred years ago, these cosmological patterns relating people to the land had already existed for thousands of years, going back to the ancient ancestors of the Pueblos. Though a community might now and again move to a new location nearer fresh fields and timber, that did not end the relationship with the land; rather, the new source of life reaffirmed belief in the renewal of their roots. For the people's bond was with the land itself, not with the homes where they lived, which were viewed merely as shelters from the weather. Indeed, except during cold weather, people mostly lived out of doors. And although, as it always must be, it was a sad wrench to leave their individual homes, the Tewa, eyeing the apparent overabundance of horses, sheep, and cattle in the Spaniards' train, and in keeping with their own naturally generous habit, may well have imagined that there might be advantages to the Spanish occupation.

VICIOUS SUBJUGATION

But the wary hope of the priesthood of possibly coming to terms with the colony was quickly shattered, and the people's lives were almost immediately badly shaken by the Spanish presence. For one of the colony's chief aims was an active program to compel the Pueblos to become Catholics. Ten friars had been assigned to the task, backed by the full force of the military. Any town that resisted this violently arrogant mission was viciously subjugated.

At the same time, soldier-colonists, unable to extract their own food and clothing from the hard land, extorted corn, beans, squash, clothing, and supplies for themselves and their livestock from the increasingly hard-pressed Pueblos—by means of wholesale torture, murder, and rape. Active resistance was immediately and savagely suppressed.

When the people of Acoma, whose adobe houseblocks were built high atop a rock mesa in western New Mexico, attacked a force led by one of Oñate's nephews, killing eleven Spaniards, including the nephew, Oñate's retaliation was swift and brutal. He stormed and burned the entire pueblo, killing in the process some five hundred men and three hundred women and children, then sentenced the survivors to twenty years of labor, and ordered every man among them over twenty-five years old to have a foot cut off.

It is difficult to credit such frank, outright, systematic brutality even at this distance. To the Pueblos, deliberate violence on a massive scale was virtually unthinkable. More and more Pueblos rebelled, and eventually most of Oñate's colonists, beginning to doubt the colony's viability, returned to Mexico. In 1606, Oñate himself was replaced, having been charged with mismanagement.

10–25,000 years ago

Inhabitants of northern Asia cross the Bering Strait to Alaska.

200–1300

The Anasazi occupy the Four Corners region of the American Southwest.

500

Celts, Basques, Libyans, and Egyptians begin sailing to the Americas, according to some archaeologists.

500–1300

Polynesians sail from the Marquesas and Tahiti Islands to the Hawaiian Islands.

700–1600

Mississippian Temple Mound Societies flourish in the American Southeast.

1000–1250

Mississippian Temple Mound culture reaches its apex at Cohokia.

1002

Leif Eriksson lands on Cape Cod.

1451

Christopher Columbus is born.

1492

Columbus begins his first voyage to the New World.

1493

Columbus embarks on his second voyage to the Americas.

1497

John Cabot sails to New England.

1498

Columbus begins his third voyage to the New World.

1499

Amerigo Vespucci sails to the New World.

1502

Columbus embarks on his fourth voyage to the Americas.

1506

Columbus dies.

1513

Ponce de León lands on the southern tip of Florida.

1519

Alonzo Alvarez de Pineda explores the Florida Gulf coast.

1520

The first epidemic of Old World diseases hits North American Indians.

1521

Ponce de León establishes a short-lived colony on his second voyage to Florida.

1524

Giovanni Verrazano explores the Atlantic coast of North America from Florida to Newfoundland.

1525

Lucas Vázquez de Ayllón explores the Atlantic coast of Florida and the Carolinas as far as Cape Fear.

1528

Pánfilo de Narváez lands in Florida; Álvar Núñez Cabeza de Vaca begins his six-year journey through the American Southwest.

1536

Cabeza de Vaca and his companions make first contact with other Spaniards and continue on to Mexico City.

1539

Hernando de Soto leads an expedition to the southeastern United States; Fray Marcos begins his journey of reconnaissance to the American Southwest.

1540

Francisco Vásquez de Coronado reaches Cíbola and battles with the Zuni; de Soto battles the Indians at Mabila; Garcia Lopez de Cardenas, a member of the Coronado expedition, becomes the first Spaniard to see the Grand Canyon.

1541

Juan Rodriquez Cabrillo leads an expedition up the California coast.

1559

Tristán de Luna de Arellano establishes a short-lived colony at Nanipacha Bay, Florida.

1564

Jean Ribault establishes the first French colony at Fort Caroline on the east coast of Florida.

1565

Pedro Menéndez de Avilés routs the French from Fort Caroline and establishes Spanish San Agustín.

1579

Francis Drake claims California for England.

1585

Ralph Lane establishes England's first colony in the Americas on Roanoke Island off the coast of North Carolina.

1586

Lane's colonists return to England.

1587

John White establishes England's second colony on Roanoke Island.

1590

White returns from England to find that his colony has vanished.

1598

Juan de Oñate establishes a colony in New Mexico.

American Heritage, *The American Heritage Book of Indians*. New York: American Heritage, 1961.

APA Productions, *Hawaii*. 4th ed. Hong Kong: APA Productions, 1983.

John Bakesless, *America as Seen by Its First Explorers*. New York: Dover, 1950.

Betty Ballantine and Ian Ballantine, eds., *The Native Americans: An Illustrated History*. Atlanta: Turner, 1993.

Lowell C. Ballard and Frank L. Beals, *Spanish Adventure Trails*. San Antonio, TX: Naylor, 1960.

John Francis Bannon, ed., *The Spanish Conquistadors: Men or Devils?* New York: Holt, Rinehart & Winston, 1960.

Morris Bishop, *The Odyssey of Cabeza de Vaca*. New York: Century, 1933.

Herbert E. Bolton, *California's Story*. Boston: Allyn and Bacon, 1922.

———, *Coronado, Knight of the Pueblos and Plains*. New York: Whittlesey House, 1949.

———, *The Spanish Borderlands: A Chronicle of Old Florida and the Southwest*. New Haven, CT: Yale University Press, 1921.

———, *Spanish Exploration of the Southwest*. New York: Charles Scribner's Sons, 1916.

Edward Gaylord Bourne, *Narratives of the Career of Hernando de Soto in the Conquest of Florida*. New York: Allerton Book, 1922.

Peter Buck, *Vikings of the Pacific*. Chicago: University of Chicago Press, 1972.

Álvar Núñez Cabeza de Vaca, *Relation of Alvar Nuñez Cabeza de Vaca*. Trans. Buckingham Smith. Ann Arbor: University Microfilms, 1966.

Bartolomé de las Casas, *The Devastation of the Indies: A Brief Account*. Trans. Herma Briffault. New York: Seabury, 1974.

Pedro Castañeda, *The Journey of Coronado*. Ann Arbor, MI: University Microfilms, 1966.

Verne E. Chatelaine, *The Defenses of Spanish Florida, 1565–1763*. Washington, DC: Carnegie Institute of Washington, 1941.

Lawrence A. Clayton, *The De Soto Chronicles: The Expedition of Hernando De Soto to North America in 1539–1543*. Tuscaloosa: University of Alabama Press, 1993.

Christopher Columbus, *The Journal of Christopher Columbus*. Trans. Cecil Jane. New York: Clarkson N. Potter, 1960.

Linda S. Cordell, *Ancient Pueblo Peoples*. New York: St. Remy/ Smithsonian Institute, 1994.

Alfred W. Crosby Jr., *The Columbian Exchange: Biological and Cultural Consequences of 1492*. Westport, CT: Greenwood, 1972.

Stephen Currie, ed., *Headlines in History: The 1500s*. San Diego: Greenhaven, 2001.

A. Grove Day, *Coronado's Quest: The Discovery of the Southwestern States*. Berkeley and Los Angeles: University of California Press, 1940.

Jean Descola, *The Conquistadors*. Trans. Malcolm Barnes. New York: Viking, 1957.

Bernard DeVoto, *The Course of Empire*. Boston: Houghton Mifflin, 1952.

Roy S. Dickens Jr., *Of Sky and Earth: Art of the Early Southeastern Indians*. Dalton, GA: Lee, 1982.

Anthony Disney, ed., *Columbus and the Consequences of 1492*. Melbourne: La Trobe University Press, 1994.

Frederick J. Dockstader, *Great North American Indians*. New York: Van Nostrand Reinhold, 1977.

Michael Dorris and Louise Erdrich, *The Crown of Columbus*. New York: HarperCollins, 1991.

David Durant, *Raleigh's Lost Colony.* London: Weidenfeld & Nicolson, 1981.

John Dyson, *Columbus: For Gold, God, and Glory.* New York: Simon and Schuster, 1991.

Margot Edmonds and Ella E. Clark, eds., *Voices of the Winds: Native American Legends.* New York: Facts On File, 1989.

Richard Erdoes and Alfonso Ortiz, eds., *American Indian Myths and Legends.* New York: Pantheon, 1984.

Don Edward Fehrenbacher, *A Basic History of California.* Princeton, NJ: Van Nostrand, 1964.

Barry Fell, *America B.C.: Ancient Settlers in the New World.* New York: Pocket Books, 1989.

Abraham Fornander, *An Account of the Polynesian Race: Its Origins and Migrations.* Rutland, VT: C.E. Tuttle, 1969.

G.P. Hammond, *New Spain and the Anglo-American West.* New York: Kraus Reprint, 1969.

G.P. Hammond and Agapito Rey, *Narratives of the Coronado Expedition, 1540–1542.* Albuquerque: New Mexico University Press, 1940.

Frederick W. Hodge, *Spanish Explorers in the Southern U.S., 1528–1543.* New York: Barnes & Noble, 1959.

Vera Brown Holmes, *A History of the Americas, from Discovery to Nationhood.* Vol. 1. New York: Ronald, 1950.

Charles M. Hudson, *Knights of Spain, Warriors of the Sun: Hernando de Soto and the South's Ancient Chiefdoms.* Athens: University of Georgia Press, 1997.

Gwyn Jones, *A History of the Vikings.* London: Oxford University Press, 1968.

Stuart A. Kallen, ed., *Headlines in History: The 1400s.* San Diego: Greenhaven, 2001.

Robert Kirsch and William S. Murphy, *West of the West: Witness to the California Experience, 1542–1906.* New York: E.P. Dutton, 1967.

Hans Koning, *Columbus: His Enterprise, Exploding the Myth.* New York: Monthly Review, 1991.

Ralph S. Kuykendall, *The Hawaiian Kingdom*. Honolulu: University of Hawaii Press, 1957.

Ralph S. Kuykendall and A. Grove Day, *Hawaii: A History, from Polynesian Kingdom to American State*. Englewood Cliffs, NJ: Prentice-Hall, 1961.

Woodbury Lowery, *The Spanish Settlements Within the Present Limits of the United States, 1513–1561*. New York: Russell & Russell, 1959.

Tristán de Luna, *The Luna Papers*. Trans. H.I. Priestley. Freeport, NY: Books for Libraries, 1971.

Peter C. Mancall, ed., *Envisioning America: English Plans for the Colonization of North America, 1580–1640*. Boston: Bedford Books, 1995.

Albert Marrin, *The Sea King: Francis Drake and His Times*. New York: Atheneum, 1995.

Theodore Maynard, *De Soto and the Conquistadors*. London: Langmans, Green, 1930.

Jerald T. Milanich and Charles Hudson, *Hernando de Soto and the Indians of Florida*. Gainesville: University of Florida Press, 1993.

Jerald T. Milanich and Susan Milbrath, *First Encounters: Spanish Explorations in the Caribbean and the U.S., 1492–1570*. Gainesville: Florida Museum of Natural History, 1989.

George R. Milner, *The Cahokia Chiefdom: The Archaeology of a Mississippian Society*. Washington, DC: Smithsonian Institution, 1998.

Samuel Eliot Morison, *Admiral of the Ocean: The Life of Christopher Columbus*. Boston: Little, Brown, 1942.

———, *A Concise History of the American Republic*. New York: Oxford University Press, 1983.

———, *The European Discovery of America: The Northern Voyages*. New York: Oxford University Press, 1974.

Timothy R. Pauketat and Thomas E. Emerson, *Cahokia: Domination and Ideology in the Mississippian World*. Lincoln: University of Nebraska Press, 1997.

David B. Quinn, ed., *North American Discovery: Circa 1000–1612*. Columbia: University of South Carolina Press, 1971.

P.H. Sawyer, *The Age of the Vikings*. New York: St. Martin's, 1962.

Edward H. Spicer, *Cycles of Conquest: The Impact of Spain, Mexico, and the U.S. on the Indians of the Southwest, 1533–1960*. Tucson: University of Arizona Press, 1962.

Ian K. Steele, *Warpaths: Invasions of North America*. New York: Oxford University Press, 1994.

H.M. Stephens and H.E. Bolton, eds., *The Pacific Ocean in History*. New York: Macmillan, 1917.

Ronald Syme, *Francisco Coronado and the Seven Cities of Gold*. New York: William Morrow, 1965.

John Upton Terrell, *Journey into Darkness*. New York: William Morrow, 1962.

Hugh Thomas, *The Story of the Atlantic Slave Trade, 1440–1870*. New York: Simon and Schuster, 1997.

Time-Life Books, *People of the Ice and Snow*. Alexandria, VA: Time-Life Books, 1994.

S. Lyman Tyler, ed., *Two Worlds: The Indian Encounters with the Europeans, 1492–1509*. Salt Lake City: University of Utah Press, 1988.

Ruth M. Underhill, *First Penthouse Dwellers of America*. New York: J.J. Augustin, 1938.

Garcilaso de la Vega, *The Florida of the Incas*. Austin: University of Texas Press, 1951.

Herman J. Viola, *After Columbus: The Smithsonian Chronicle of the North American Indians*. Washington, DC: Smithsonian Books, 1990.

David J. Weber, *The Spanish Frontier in North America*. New Haven, CT: Yale University Press, 1992.

Justin Winsor, *Narrative and Critical History of America*. Boston: Houghton Mifflin, 1889.

Henry Woodhead, *The European Challenge: The American Indians*. Alexandria, VA: Time-Life Books, 1992.

Lawrence C. Wroth, *The Voyages of Giovanni da Verrazzano, 1524–1528.* New Haven, CT: Yale University Press, 1970.

Bill Yenne, *The Encyclopedia of North America Indian Tribes: A Comprehensive Study of Tribes from the Abitibi to the Zuni.* New York: Crescent Books, 1986.

John Yewell, Chris Dodge, and Jan DeSirey, eds., *Confronting Columbus: An Anthology.* Jefferson, NC: McFarland, 1992.

INDEX